W9-AUW-652

Chinese Soul Food

中華民廚

Chinese Soul Food

A Friendly Guide for Homemade Dumplings, Stir-Fries, Soups, and More

HSIAO-CHING CHOU

Photography by Clare Barboza

SASQUATCH BOOKS
SEATTLE

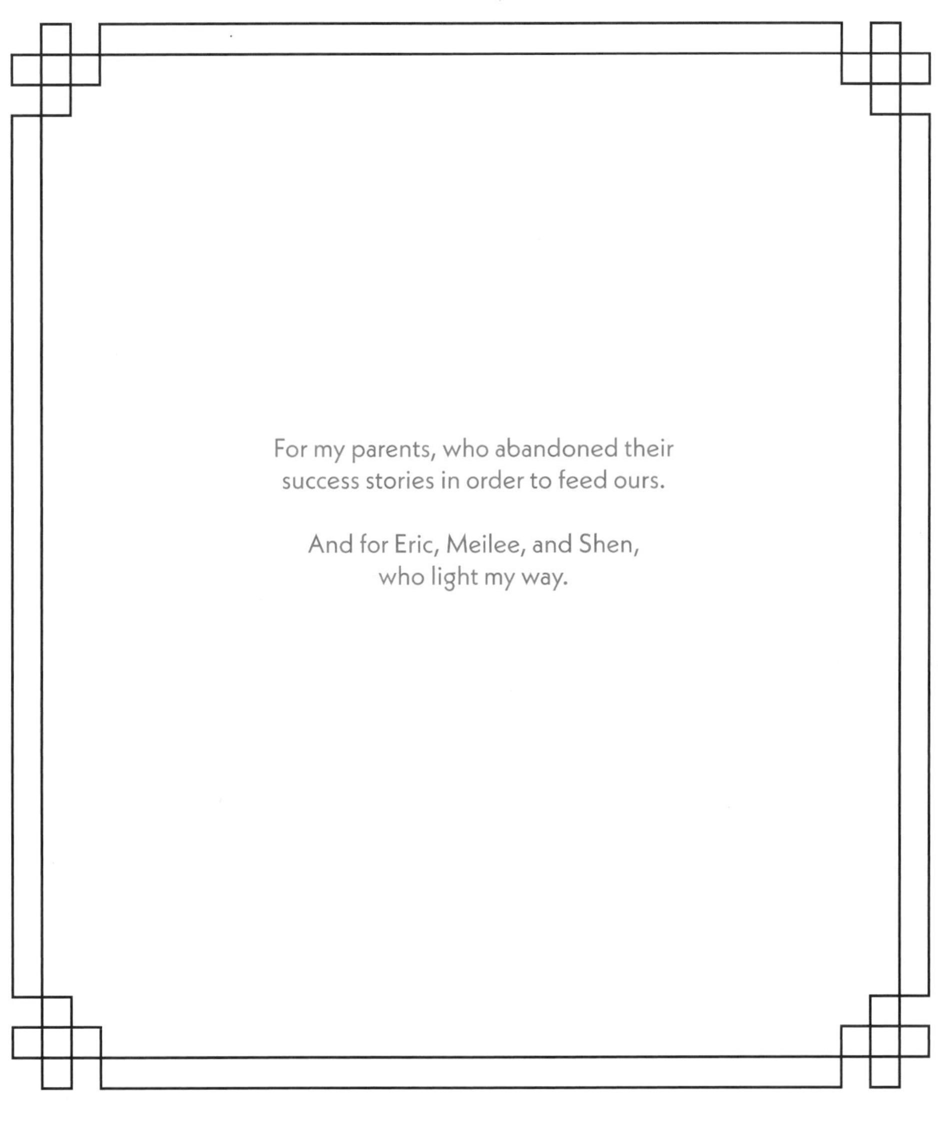

For my parents, who abandoned their
success stories in order to feed ours.

And for Eric, Meilee, and Shen,
who light my way.

Recipe List

序愛女曉晴新書　　　　　　　　　　　　周徐喚民
～～深藏於心的家常料理

曉晴的書讓我聯想到中國俗語「小菜一碟」。它的英文巧對是「蛋糕一塊」！都是形容：在美式廚房做中國菜沒什麼難的。

一般華人家庭很少有人帶本食譜進廚房。除了年節，大多是有啥吃啥，隨遇而安。我沒有食譜，我母親也沒有。

有天，我第一次下廚給自己做了碗蝦仁蘿蔔絲米粉湯。那是因為媽不在家。通常廚房是我的禁地，我媽從小沒上過學常恨自己不識字，最大的願望就是我能接受完整的學校教育，不願我因為做飯耽誤功課。雖然我從來沒想過要做學問，卻為了母親跑到美國密蘇里掙了個碩士學位。

先父畢生軍旅，收入不豐。幸賴軍眷補給全家未受凍餓。我誕生於中日戰亂年代，童年生活乏善可陳，竟然找不到一張照片證明我曾存在。

也因此養成我隨緣豁達的性情，少期盼、多感恩。

完成母親最大的心願之後，我回國嫁給大學同班周長生。我們都有穩定職業和收，小家庭添了女兒曉晴和大兒子士弘。當長生準備繼續進修時，我們帶著兩個孩子來到美國住進有眷學生公寓，接收了一些學長留下的鍋碗瓢盆，我才正式走進廚房。沒有炒鍋，先生鋸了丨段掃把給我當擀麵棍。小兒子士毅在大學醫院誕生。

我依據的「食譜」是記憶中的美食，追尋的是深藏於心的味道。我常自矖為「印象派」。

直到開了第一家外賣餐館才買了一本食譜來印證一些細節問題。

曉晴在書中喚回許多家庭裡關於食的記憶，溫馨、美好，都與山珍海味無關。她解釋這本書的初衷就是由簡單著手，帶你走進廚房。因為一個溫暖的廚房才是家的心房。

下廚很簡單。我們是過來人。

Foreword

In *The Primrose Path* in 1936, Ogden Nash writes, "Her picture's in the papers now, and life's a piece of cake."

While reading my daughter Hsiao-Ching's cookbook, I thought about this quote because her message, ultimately, is that cooking Chinese food in a Western kitchen is not as hard as it may seem. Most Chinese people go into their kitchens without ever consulting a cookbook. I don't. My mother certainly didn't.

The very first dish I ever cooked for myself was a bowl of rice noodle soup with daikon radish strips and a few pieces of dried shrimp for flavor. It was only because my mother was not home that day that I had to feed myself. The kitchen was normally off-limits to me. The wok was there, and the stove was there, but my mother never let me touch them. Her biggest regret was that her circumstances prevented her from attending school, so her dream was for me to complete my formal education. She didn't want me wasting my time in the kitchen. So, even though I had no ambition for becoming an academic, I reached graduate school and earned a master's degree (from the University of Missouri School of Journalism) for her.

My father was a military man with a limited income. Luckily, our family received a small stipend for military dependents that helped. I was born during the Sino-Japanese War, and I didn't even have a single photo to prove my existence. Thus, my character was built on the value of not asking for too much in life and appreciating whatever I may receive.

After I fulfilled my mother's dream, I married a man I'd met in college. We both had steady jobs and fair incomes, so we started a family and had Hsiao-Ching first, then her brother, Shih-Hung. When my husband decided to pursue his master's degree (also at the University of Missouri), we set forth on our future life in the United States.

With my husband in school and two young children in tow, I eventually gave up my career as a journalist. That was when I started taking cooking more seriously. We were in a campus apartment with some hand-me-down cookware, but no wok. But I tried every way to feed my family, including making dumpling skins with a sawed-off broomstick as a rolling pin. Our third child, David Jr., was born at University Hospital near campus.

The only "cookbook" I always had was my memory of good eating. So I joked that I was an "impressionist" cook. It wasn't until we opened a small carryout restaurant that I even bought a Chinese cookbook to double-check some details related to techniques.

Hsiao-Ching explains that the purpose of this book is to encourage people to get into the kitchen and start cooking. That's what we did, and so can you. I am mostly touched by the fond family memories she has brought back with her stories. A warm kitchen is the heart of the family. And that is sweeter than cake.

—ELLEN CHOU

Introduction

Growing up in my family's Chinese restaurant and then becoming a professional food writer did not give me license to write a cookbook. I had the ingredients, so to speak: an immigrant story, restaurant credibility, a journalism degree, a food column in the *Seattle Post-Intelligencer* newspaper, a fan base, an agent, even polite interest from a couple of New York publishers. But I had nothing to say.

It wasn't until after I had gotten married, had two children, quit the newspaper, and changed career paths a couple of times that the cookbook declared to me its need to exist. Life had taken me on the scenic route toward this end, and it began with the Chinese Soul Food blog in 2007, which I had started in hopes of maintaining my weekly practice of writing and providing a hub for my fans. I also wanted to create a space to share straightforward but comforting recipes inspired by foods I ate growing up. The ingredients wouldn't break the bank, and the recipes could be made, possibly, with a small child literally wrapped around your leg or while wearing a baby in a sling. That scenario was a reality for me at the time. Money was tight too, so I had to be resourceful about ingredients. I knew that the Chinese cooking I had grown up eating could be extremely economical, considering many stir-fries are vegetable-centric with meat only as a condiment. I figured if I needed such a resource, there probably were other parents out there in the same boat. Despite a good start, the blog suffered from neglect, especially after I had a second child. So it went dormant until 2015, when the opportunity to teach regular classes on Chinese cooking at Hot Stove Society, an avocational cooking school in Seattle, revived my need for a recipe blog.

When I was at the newspaper, my column was a weekly trigger for home cooks to reach out to me with questions or comments about recipes of all types. I learned as much from the readers as they learned from me. After I left the paper, that channel of exchange became nonexistent. It took five or so years away from the day to day of journalism to give me the perspective I needed to understand what I had missed about being a columnist: telling universal stories through the lens of cooking, eating, and thinking about food—and, more importantly, being in a position to convey cooking skills to a broad audience in order to empower them to feed themselves and their families deliciously, simply, and wholesomely. I knew that

I needed to return to the food community in some way to regain that connection with home cooks. Through monthly cooking classes on how to make pot stickers, soup dumplings, and simple stir-fries, the path back into the conversation opened up again.

My ultimate goal is to get you into the kitchen. Chinese cooking can be daunting because the ingredients and methods are unfamiliar, and, if you haven't experienced the diversity of regional Chinese dishes, your palate may not have a baseline for the flavor profiles. The complaints I hear most often about why people don't cook Chinese food are that the ingredients seem too "exotic" and that cutting all the ingredients is so much work. The most common "aha" I hear after students attend a class, however, is that a given dish wasn't as hard to cook as they thought. Even one of my chef colleagues at the cooking school, for example, commented that she was surprised at how accessible—and delicious—many of my recipes are. I think our brains are wired to associate long lists of ingredients with a higher degree of difficulty, causing us to see a greater challenge than exists. I make it a point to remind all the home cooks I meet to have a growth mind-set: You will likely have some "mess ups" to start, and that's okay. You will improve only if you first develop a *habit* of cooking Chinese dishes. When you internalize some of the basic principles, you will be able to improvise based on what's available. Chinese cooks, in general, don't start with a recipe or menu. They are more likely to let the ingredients on hand, and any leftovers, determine what they cook. They are more concerned with balancing the components and flavors of a meal than following a particular recipe. Perhaps your journey starts with cooking a Chinese meal once a week and building from there. Don't fret about not having the exact equipment or the full complement of specialty ingredients. Yes, having appropriate equipment, in general, makes it easier to cook. But, ultimately, Chinese home cooking is about being resourceful and adaptable. Any kitchen can be a Chinese kitchen.

When my parents first arrived in Columbia, Missouri, in 1975 with two young children and a few suitcases, there were no Asian markets. They had to shop at IGA, Schnucks, and Kroger, where they couldn't even find napa cabbage or any other familiar ingredients. They had to drive ten hours north to Chicago to stock up on good soy sauce. We had secondhand cookware and a humble food budget. We lived in a tiny apartment in a university-owned complex for graduate and married students. And yet, my parents cooked Chinese meals every day.

It's this food that sustained me in those early formative years. I have clear memories of being four or five years old, standing on my toes trying to watch my mother make dumplings; of slurping too-hot chicken soup with ginger and shiitakes while sitting at our white metal dinner table; of eating bowls of rice topped

A WORD ON RECIPE YIELDS AND MEAL PLANNING

A typical meal consists of several complementary dishes, served family style with enough steamed rice for everyone. When planning a meal, consider the balance of flavors, textures, colors, types of ingredients, and cooking methods. If you are serving a rich, tender, meaty dish, such as Red-Braised Pork Belly (page 187), you want to provide a counterpoint, such as crisp and fresh Simple Stir-Fried Greens (page 137). If you serve Ma Po Tofu (page 148), which is spicy and numbing, you may want to pair it with a mild and, perhaps, slightly sweet dish, such as Dry-Fried Green Beans (page 147)—and plenty of steamed rice. Choose dishes of varying cooking methods so that you have something cold or room temperature, something braised that can hold on the back burner, and something stir-fried that requires last-minute cooking. This way, you aren't chained to the stove. While soups can be served at the beginning of a meal, it's common for soup to arrive at the end of dinner to wash everything down.

with red-braised pork; of the very special occasions when my father would splurge for frozen Alaskan snow crab to stir-fry with green onions, ginger, and garlic. I also can hear the dull sound of wooden chopsticks tapping the bottom of the small aluminum pot that my parents used to make rice, soup, and even the Kung-Fu brand instant noodles that, to this day, I will eat on occasion.

By the time my parents opened a restaurant in 1980, it was easier to get Asian ingredients in Columbia. There were specialty wholesalers in Saint Louis that would send their trucks an hour and a half to our town to deliver to us and the other Chinese restaurants. Having access to authentic ingredients did not mitigate our customers' demands for deep-fried sweet-and-sour pork, cream cheese wontons, chop suey, cashew chicken, and the like. They wanted cheap and fast Chinese food that satisfied their sweet tooth. During the twenty-three years the restaurant operated, the turning point came in the mid-1990s when my parents pivoted from full-service dining to a buffet restaurant. Business increased substantially, which certainly benefited the family, but while much of the menu reflected Americanized dishes, we billed ourselves as a home-style Sichuanese restaurant. We offered classic dishes, such as ma po tofu, dry-fried green beans, fish-fragrant eggplant, kung pao chicken, and twice-cooked pork. These were far from best sellers, but they were dishes my parents liked that reminded them of home. Neither of them were born in the Sichuan Province in China, however. Their palates were shaped by war.

My mother's family was from the north in Manchuria and my father's family was from Henan in central China. Because my grandfathers were both officers in the Kuomintang's National Army, they and their families retreated to Taiwan when the Communists took over in 1949. All the mainlander military families settled in what initially were meant to be provisional villages throughout the island. The culinary result of this displacement of people from diverse regions across China who now were surrounded by Taiwanese culture was a delicious intersection of influences on home cooking. This thread carried through to our family's restaurant. The Chinese name my parents coined for the restaurant translates roughly to "homeland cooking" or "home-style eats."

Similarly, the Chinese name for this cookbook loosely translates to "Everyone's Kitchen." The spirit of the name connects to the heart of the cooking in this book, which is grounded in this legacy of intertwined regional traditions and resourcefulness. I can take small liberties to accommodate taste preferences or apply refinements to the techniques and choice of ingredients, but the recipes all have humble origins. Comfort comes in the tingling *ma la* (or "numbing spice") of Sichuanese ma po tofu, the nuance of northern steamed dumplings, the caramelized richness of Taiwanese braised beef noodle soup. It isn't high cuisine. It is Chinese food for the soul.

Key Ingredients, Techniques, and Equipment

Ingredients

Asian markets aren't all the same. Consider how many Asian cultures and countries there are. For example, there are several national chains of Asian markets including 99 Ranch Market (Chinese), H Mart (Korean), and Seafood City Supermarket (Filipino). While many produce, meat, and seafood items may overlap, there are numerous more ingredients that are specific to the cuisine, culture, and geography. I cannot find my preferred soy sauces or familiar Chinese brands of condiments at H Mart or Seafood City. If I want to make Korean-style kalbi short ribs, however, or explore a mind-blowing spectrum of kimchis, H Mart offers that in spades. Similarly, Seafood City speaks its own language when it comes to Filipino brands and has a stunning variety of seafood, especially whole fish. My general rule of thumb is that if you are looking for ingredients to cook Chinese foods, then you'll have better luck at a Chinese-centric market.

If you are a novice, there are a few must-have pantry items you'll need to get started: good-quality soy sauce, sesame oil, rice vinegar, Chinese chili sauce, chili bean paste, hoisin sauce, oyster sauce, rice wine or dry Marsala wine, white pepper powder, and dried shiitake mushrooms. With this selection as a foundation, you can make any number of dishes. If you add Chinese rock candy (sugar), Sichuan peppercorns, and star anise, your pantry will be set for red braising and some of the spicy Sichuanese dishes.

For many pantry items and specialty cooking equipment, Amazon is a great resource—especially if you don't live near an Asian market. Wokshop.com is also a must for cooking equipment and tools, and you can also visit MyChineseSoulFood.com to see up-to-date shopping information.

Any Asian market will overwhelm you by the sheer number of products available. The diversity of soy sauces alone is staggering. These days, even neighborhood grocery stores, recognizing that their shoppers are more diverse in their demands, offer many of the basics you would need to make most of the recipes in this book. There are a few specialty items that are best sought at an Asian market, where the selection is better and/or less expensive. What follows are the ingredients that I stock in my kitchen regularly. I excluded common spices, such as cinnamon, clove, cumin, and fennel, which you probably already have in your pantry.

Aromatics

GINGER: Fresh ginger is a staple and adds zing to many dishes. It counterbalances the strong flavors of meat or seafood. It also helps to settle the stomach. Look for plump gingerroot that has smooth, succulent skin. If it's wrinkled, it means it's dried up. **Prep:** The general rules for ginger in this book: There is no need to peel the ginger when the recipe calls for slices. But peel the ginger if the recipe calls for grated or minced ginger. I'm not one to use squeeze-tube ginger paste, because you don't get the texture of hand-cut ginger and the flavor isn't as fresh. In a pinch, ginger paste would work for making a dipping sauce.

GARLIC: Look for bulbs of garlic that have bright skins and firm cloves. Avoid ones that have brown spots, feel soft, or have green sprouts in the middle. **Prep:** For many recipes in this book, you can mince, crush, or smash the garlic as specified.

GREEN ONIONS: Also known as "scallions," green onions are ubiquitous in Chinese cooking. They're often combined with ginger and garlic to increase the pungency of dishes. **Prep:** For the recipes in this book, use both the white and green parts of the stalk. Cut off the root end, and if the greens have any brown edges, trim them off.

RICE WINE: There are two main types of rice wine that are used in Chinese cooking to add fragrance to marinades, stir-fries, and braises. Taiwanese-style michiu (*mi*, or "rice," and *chiu*, or "alcohol") is clear in color and made by distillation. Shaoxing wine is amber colored and originates from the Shaoxing region in China. Shaoxing wine is brewed from partially steamed and fermented glutinous rice, and aged in large ceramic urns. Unfortunately, many of the widely available Shaoxing wines in the States are labeled "cooking wine" and may contain salt. Avoid this. I usually look for higher quality versions in the wine aisle at an Asian market. An ideal substitute is a decent-quality dry Marsala wine or a sherry. Of course, I always say that if you need a splash of wine for a dish, you can always use whatever bottle of everyday wine you happen to have open.

Shaoxing wine has a long history and much cultural significance. The earliest reference to this "yellow wine" appears around 470 BC. It was frequently used as an incentive in various political and business dealings, as well as a revenue source for the local government. The rice wine from Shaoxing is particularly revered due to the quality of the water from Jianhu Lake—also called Mirror Lake because of its mirror-like surface—that's used in brewing (*Jianhu* means "rivers and lakes"). Shaoxing wine can be aged from three years to more than one hundred. The most common type of Shaoxing is called *hua diao* or *hua tiao chiew*, which refers to the flowery designs carved into the wine urns. Modernized factory breweries use amber bottles. The five main grades of Shaoxing range in alcohol content from about 14 to 24 percent. The wine is meant to be sipped lukewarm and with appetizers; it typically isn't served with the main meal. The best aged Shaoxing wines are reserved for celebrating milestones. It once was customary to store hua diao on the birth of a daughter and then include it as part of her dowry as wine for the wedding. *Nu er hong* (*nu er*, or "daughter," and *hong*, or "red wine") appears on ornately packaged Shaoxing wines meant as gifts. The flavor of Shaoxing wine is described as nutty, fragrant, mushroomy, and smoky. To the unaccustomed palate, such as mine, Shaoxing wine is harsh. I don't find it enjoyable as a table wine.

SICHUAN PEPPERCORN: These reddish-brown peppercorns are called prickly ash and are essential in Sichuan recipes. Sichuan peppercorns are fragrant and cause a tingling sensation on your tongue, especially when combined with chili sauce or hot oil. There is no substitute for Sichuan peppercorns. If you can't get to an Asian market, visit a spice shop or the bulk spice section at your market. There are many online sources for spices, including Amazon.com, Kalustyans.com, and MarxFoods.com. There is a green variety, which has a pine-like flavor, but the recipes in this book call for the red variety. **Prep:** In a dry skillet over medium heat, toast the peppercorns for 3 to 4 minutes, stirring frequently, before using. I like to keep a separate pepper mill filled with toasted Sichuan peppercorns so that I can freshly crack them into dishes, such as Ma Po Tofu (page 148) or Orange Beef (page 159).

STAR ANISE: The licorice-flavored spice should be used sparingly. But it is an essential component to many braised dishes, such as Red-Braised Pork Belly (page 187) or Sliced Red-Braised Beef Shank (page 189). It's far less expensive to buy star anise at an Asian market. Store it in an airtight container, and it'll keep in the pantry indefinitely.

WHITE PEPPER POWDER: White pepper is aged and fermented, which gives it a floral, nuanced heat. It is generally not interchangeable with black pepper. I buy bottled ground white pepper from Asian markets because the texture of the pepper is finer and more powderlike than freshly ground white pepper. (In Chinese, we call it "white pepper powder," even though the translated labels don't use the term "powder.") It will last for months in the pantry. **Prep:** If you buy whole white peppercorns, then grind 2 to 3 tablespoons in a spice grinder until very fine. This will yield more than enough to season a few meals. Keep in a small jar with a lid.

Oils

CHILI OIL: Chili oil usually is made by heating a neutral-flavored oil and adding it to ground red chili peppers or crushed red pepper. Sometimes, other spices, such as Sichuan peppercorns, may be included. You can buy bottled chili oil at the store, but it will be fresher if you make your own (see page 99).

PEANUT OIL: China is the top producer of peanuts in the world, so peanut oil is common in Chinese cooking. While it has nice flavor and a high smoke point, peanut oil is not required to make the recipes in this book.

SESAME OIL: Treat sesame oil as a finishing touch on dishes to add a beautiful toasted, nutty flavor. Sesame oil is not meant to be used as a cooking oil. The oil can be made from white or black sesame seeds. Asian sesame oils tend to be made from toasted sesame seeds, which yield its amber color. Some makers of sesame oil offer a less expensive version that's diluted with vegetable oil, which softens the aroma. Pure sesame oil tastes better, however.

VEGETABLE OIL: A generic vegetable, soybean, canola, or neutral-flavored oil works well for cooking. Oils that have strong, distinctive flavors—such as coconut oil or olive oil—can clash with Chinese flavor profiles.

Dried Ingredients

DRIED KELP: Kelp is used in soups, salads, and stir-fries. You can buy it in larger sheets or cut into bite-size squares. Having precut pieces makes it easier to drop them directly into soups. **Prep:** If you have kelp sheets, soak the kelp in warm tap water for about 30 minutes, or until softened enough to cut into the desired size or shape.

DRIED RED CHILI PEPPERS: Look for the japones chile. It's often labeled generically as "red chili pepper" in Asian markets. Dried chile de arbol is another option, if you can't find the japones chile. **Prep:** If stir-frying, add the chili at the beginning while the cooking oil is heating to activate the flavor, but do not let it burn or it will become acrid.

DRIED SHRIMP: In Asian markets, you'll find dried shrimp in a range of diminutive sizes, shelled or unshelled, head on or headless. They are used as a pungent flavor component in fillings, stir-fries, soups, and stews. Chinese cabbage with dried shrimp is a classic combination. **Prep:** Rinse the dried shrimp in cold water, then soak in warm tap water for 1 to 2 hours to reconstitute. Drain before using.

DRIED SHIITAKE MUSHROOMS: Dried shiitake come in different varieties and sizes. The more prized types are small, thick, and have a crackle-like pattern on the cap. They're called *hua gu,* which translates to "flower mushroom," and can be expensive. The other, more utilitarian type of shiitake is called *xiang gu*, or "fragrant mushroom." The caps are thinner, darker, and smoother. I prefer the fragrant shiitake for the intense, savory-mushroom (umami) flavor they add to soups and stir-fries. **Prep:** Soak the mushrooms in cool water for at least 2 hours, or until reconstituted.

DRIED TANGERINE PEEL: Dried tangerine peel is often used in herbal remedies, but it's also used in making Orange Beef (page 159). You can find dried tangerine peel in Asian markets or medicine shops. **Prep:** Soak the tangerine peel for 20 to 30 minutes in warm water to rehydrate. Gently scrape off any white pith with a knife, if needed.

DRIED WOOD EAR FUNGUS: This crunchy fungus is used in soups and stir-fries. It has a mild flavor and adds great texture. **Prep:** Soak in cool water for 2 hours, or until reconstituted. If whole, trim the stem end and cut into desired size. Precut strips can be used right away.

FRIED SHALLOTS: Fried shallots add great flavor to soups, buns, and any other dish where the flavor needs a boost. They're widely available in large packs or plastic jars at Asian markets. To guarantee freshness, it's best to make your own (see page 188).

RED CHILI POWDER: Chinese chili powder is ideal for making chili oil. A Korean chili powder, typically used to make kimchi, is an alternative. Asian-style chili powders contain only chili. Western-style chili powders often contain other spices.

Sauces and Pastes

BEAN SAUCE OR PASTE: Made from fermented yellow soybeans, this paste is used in a variety of dishes. It's also an ingredient in hoisin sauce and the sauce served with Chinese barbecued duck.

Is it a sauce or a paste? In Chinese, the word *jiang* covers both "sauce" and "paste." The English translation on product labels isn't consistent from brand to brand. I use "sauce" and "paste" interchangeably, except when referring to types of soy sauces. Soy sauce is more liquid and briny, and soy paste is thickened and sweetened soy sauce.

CHILI BEAN PASTE OR SAUCE: The original chili bean paste comes from Pixian region in the Sichuan Province in China. The sauce is made from fermented chilies and fava beans and is distinctive for its quality of flavor. Other chili bean pastes may contain soybeans and additional flavorings, and may not be as spicy. Which you think is best will depend on your preference. The Sichuan Pixian Douban Co.'s authentic chili bean sauce is now available in the United States and can be found in Chinese markets or online. (If needed, you can chop up any larger chunks in the Pixian chili bean paste.) Lee Kum Kee, a widely available brand, makes chili bean paste that contains both fava beans and soybeans.

CHILI SAUCE: There are many different brands of chili sauce that have varying degrees of spiciness. It can be fun to collect and experiment with different types. In general, choose a chili sauce that has no sugar or minimal sugar. Some chili sauces contain garlic, fermented black beans, and/or a healthy layer of chili oil. Note that fermented black beans add funkiness and saltiness, so adjust the seasonings in your dish as necessary.

HOISIN SAUCE: This sauce is made from yellow beans, sugar, vinegar, salt, and many other seasonings (depending on the manufacturer's recipe). It's often used as a condiment or mixed with other sauces to flavor stir-fries.

OYSTER SAUCE: This is a thick sauce made with oyster extract, soy sauce, and other seasonings. It's Cantonese in origin and often used in stir-fries or as a condiment.

SA CHA: This sauce is also called Chinese barbecue sauce. It's made with dried fish and shrimp and a mix of spices. It can be combined with other sauces to add complexity. You also can add it to hot pot broth to give it a kick. There are many varieties, but the Bull Head brand, which comes in a silver tin, is popular.

NEW
Fermented Beancurd
INGREDIENTS: SOYABEAN, WATER, SALT, WINE, RED RICE
NET WT. 16 OZ (1 LB.) or 454 GRAMS
東湖
SODIUM FREE • SUGAR FREE
Marukan
SINCE 1649
GENUINE BREWE
RiceVineg
12 FL OZ (355mL)
ALL NATURAL
李錦記
LEE KUM KEE
香豉
辣椒醬
CHILI BLACK
BEAN SAUCE
NET WT. 8.1 oz (230 g)
李錦記
LEE KUM KEE
海鮮醬
HOISIN
SAUCE
TƯƠNG ĂN PHỞ
绍兴
FAMILY
100%
SESAME OI
純正芝麻油
THIS PRODUCT CONTAINS NO PRESERV
辣豆瓣醬
CHILI BEAN SAUCE

SOY SAUCE: Soy sauces vary from cuisine to cuisine in flavor profile. A Japanese shoyu that's meant for sashimi, for example, is not appropriate for stir-fries. As a general rule, I tell people to buy Chinese soy sauce for Chinese cooking. Look for soy sauce that's naturally fermented and brewed. Avoid bottles that list "hydrolyzed soy protein" as an ingredient, because that would be akin to buying maple syrup made from corn syrup and maple flavoring. Chinese soy sauces may include designations such as "light," "dark," "thick," "paste," and "aged." Light soy sauce does not refer to the calorie count; it refers to the color and viscosity. Light soy sauce tends to be saltier. The less salty darker or thicker sauces are typically used for braises. Aged soy sauces have an intense flavor that may be an acquired taste.

SWEET BEAN PASTE OR SAUCE: There is a slight confusion about this sauce. In Mandarin, it's called *tian mian jiang*, or "sweet flour sauce." It's made with flour, sugar, salt, and fermented yellow soybeans leftover from making soy sauce. It is used to flavor and thicken various sauces for noodles or stir-fries, such as Chinese Noodles in Meat Sauce (Zha Jiang Mian) (page 123) and Mongolian Beef (page 229).

Umami and Funky Fermented

FERMENTED TOFU OR BEAN CURD: Fermented tofu is pungent and has a funky flavor akin to stinky cheese. It's most often served as a condiment for Simple Congee (page 118), but it's a great addition in marinades, where its pungency enhances the overall flavor but is also tamed by other ingredients. Look for jars of fermented tofu in the refrigerated section of Asian markets. This is different from the red fermented bean curd (see page 30).

PRESERVED DUCK EGG: Also called century egg or thousand-year-old egg, this preserved duck egg turns dark and pungent after it's fermented. You can get the yolks in varying degrees of softness. I look for brands made in Taiwan, and I personally like eggs that have a soft yolk. The eggs often come in packs of four or six. They're individually wrapped in strong plastic. Beware that when you cut open the plastic, it can release some pungent aromas. Before discarding the shells, you might consider sealing them in a recycled produce bag, or, if you compost, take the shells directly outside to the compost bin. **Prep:** Peel and cut the egg into quarters and drizzle with soy sauce and sesame oil.

UNDERSTANDING SOY SAUCE

I have done organized tastings of dozens of soy sauces and researched scientific papers on the flavor components of soy sauces to build a better vocabulary for describing the flavor profiles of soy sauces, the quintessential ingredient not only in Chinese cooking but across all Asian cuisines. Through mass spectrometry, scientists have identified at least eighty volatile components—such as alcohols, acids, and esters—in soy sauce that contribute to its flavor. Out of the eighty components, around thirty are common across most soy sauces. The individuality of a given soy sauce is the result of the type of soybeans, the geographical and environmental conditions (terroir), the type of yeast, and the particulars of the fermentation and brewing process. Researchers identified compounds that yield "malty," "caramel," "roselike," "smoky," "sweaty," and "baked-potato" aromas.

In one tasting session, a sommelier friend helped me identify other flavor notes in a cross section of eighteen soy sauces that ranged from "all purpose" to one that had been aged for twelve years. We tasted them straight from the bottle as well as heated over high heat in a wok (to mimic stir-frying). Our tasting notes include descriptors such as "earthy," "molasses," "floral," "meaty beef broth," "juicy," "nutty," and "mushroom." For an ingredient that is an afterthought to many home cooks, this exercise is useful in my efforts to expand our collective understanding of the essence of Chinese cooking.

My current go-to naturally brewed soy sauces are:

- Kimlan, green label, low sodium for its fruitiness
- Wei-Chuan, gold label, premium for its rich, broth-like flavor
- Kimlan, yellow label for my "all-purpose" needs

RED FERMENTED BEAN CURD OR TOFU: This tofu is made with red yeast rice, which gives it its distinctive color. This is typically used in marinades for meats, such as for Chinese Barbecued Pork (page 239). As a shortcut, many Chinese restaurants or barbecue shops add red dye to their marinades to mimic the color that traditionally comes from red fermented bean curd. This is unfortunate. Luckily, red fermented bean curd is available in some Asian markets in the refrigerated aisle and online.

Acid

PICKLED CHINESE MUSTARD GREENS: This is often used as a condiment for noodles or different types of steamed buns. It also can be used in soups and stir-fries. The pickled greens come in a plastic, shelf-stable pouch and usually can be found in the dry goods aisle at Asian markets. Sometimes, you'll find them in the refrigerated section. There are Chinese and Thai brands, some of which add food coloring to "brighten" up the look. **Prep:** You also can ferment your own (see page 157). Rinse the greens before using.

RICE VINEGAR: Rice vinegars are made from fermented glutinous rice. The most beloved Chinese variety is called Zhenjiang or Chinkiang vinegar and is amber or black in color. It is more pungent than golden, milder rice vinegars. If you can't find Zhenjiang black vinegar, you can use everyday balsamic vinegar. Unseasoned Japanese rice vinegar is more widely available and is fine to use for the dipping-sauce recipes in this book.

Sweet

CHINESE SAUSAGE: Chinese sausage is usually made from pork and unrendered fat and has a sweet flavor. The sausage may be dried or fresh and can be smoked. Some varieties are seasoned with rice wine and may contain liver. It's common to see Chinese sausage referred to as *lap cheong*, its Cantonese name. There are many brands of Chinese sausage, but a common one that's even available at warehouse clubs is Kam Yen Jen. Venus brand "cured Chinese-style sweet sausage" is reliable too. If you live near a Chinatown, you may be able to find locally made sausages. **Prep:** Cook the sausage either by steaming it whole or slicing and browning it in a pan before eating or incorporating into other dishes.

ROCK SUGAR: Also called "rock candy," this is crystallized sugar made from liquid brown sugar. It is available in large, jagged pieces that must be broken into smaller chunks. A hammer, mallet, or pestle is handy for this task. Rock sugar is also available in lozenge-like pieces, which are easier to handle. Rock candy adds sheen to the sauces for red-braised dishes. If you can't find rock sugar, use dark brown sugar instead.

A WORD ON DESSERTS

The Chinese usually serve fresh fruit after a meal instead of desserts, which are enjoyed more as snacks. Chinese desserts tend to be less sweet and frequently feature red bean, lotus, black sesame paste, dates, and tropical fruits. Herbal and fruit jellies are common. Shaved ice topped with fresh fruit, red bean compote, and jellies is a beloved hot-weather refresher. Layer cakes tend to be airy in texture and filled with fresh fruit—it can be a shock to the Western palate to take a bite of birthday cake and sink your teeth into a piece of honeydew melon! I love making cakes, pies, and other desserts as occasional treats for my family, or when I'm entertaining guests. But I don't typically serve desserts after a Chinese meal, so you won't find any recipes for sweets in this book. The one exception, however, is for Almond Jelly with Fruit Cocktail (page 240) in the last chapter. Since the recipes in that chapter reflect the Americanized menu of my family's restaurant, I thought it would be fun to include a touch of kitsch.

RED FERMENTED TOFU

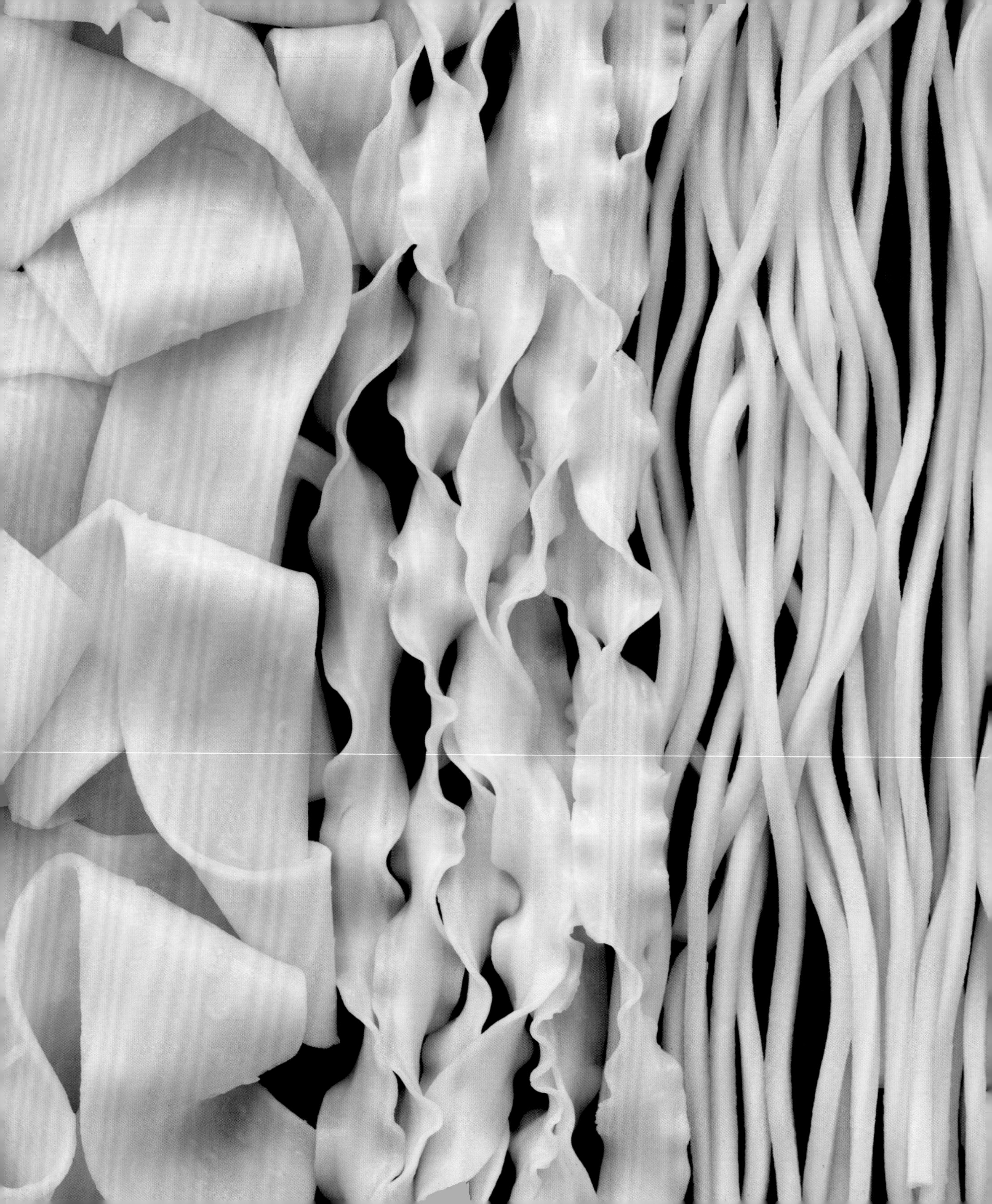

Rice and Noodles

BEAN THREAD NOODLES: Also called cellophane, glass, vermicelli, maifun, or saifun noodles, bean thread noodles are made out of mung bean starch and potato starch. Be sure to look for the term "bean thread" somewhere on the package, because there's also rice vermicelli, or "rice stick," which resembles bean thread. Soak the bundle of noodles in warm tap water for 10 minutes, or until pliable. Bean thread noodles appear most frequently in soups, but they're also delicious in stir-fries. In Asian markets, it's common to see bean thread in packs of eight small bundles that are wrapped in a garish pink net bag. They store indefinitely in the cabinet.

***CHOW FUN* OR *HE FEN*:** These fresh rice noodles come either precut or in large sheets that you can cut to the desired width. Asian markets that sell fresh rice noodles usually make them in house or get them from a nearby noodle factory. You have to buy them the same day for the best quality or they become hard and more challenging to handle. Dynasty brand does sell *chow fun* noodles sealed in plastic pouches that can be found in the refrigerated noodle aisle of Asian markets. They oil the noodles profusely to keep them from sticking and drying out.

EGG ROLL WRAPPERS: Egg roll wrappers are as widely available as wonton skins. Use them within a couple of days of purchase or freeze them and defrost as needed.

RICE: There are many types and brands of rice. What you buy will be based on taste preference and price. Most rices available in US markets—even Asian brands—are likely grown in California or Arkansas. Jasmine is a good all-purpose long-grain rice that has a lovely floral aroma and is widely available. Long-grain rices are drier and stay loose when cooked. I personally like short- or medium-grain rice, which is starchier and stickier. The nuttiness of brown rice is great on its own or in fried rice. Glutinous rice is a sweet rice that's usually used for *zong zi* (a Chinese tamale) or sticky rice in lotus leaf.

RICE NOODLES: Dried rice vermicelli noodles, or "rice stick," resemble angel-hair pasta in fineness; they're usually sold in one-pound packages. It's most common to stir-fry these noodles, though they're delicious in soups too. Fresh rice noodles are called *he fen* or *ho fun*. They can be purchased in sheets or in precut widths. **Prep:** Soak the dried rice noodles in warm tap water for 10 to 15 minutes until pliable.

SPRING ROLL WRAPPERS: These square, crepe-like wrappers are used for making delicately crispy spring rolls. They are sold frozen and are not to be confused with the Vietnamese-style round spring roll wrappers, which are dried. Wei-Chuan or Spring Home brands are widely available. Defrost overnight in the refrigerator before using.

WHEAT NOODLES: The number of styles of dried and fresh noodles can be dizzying. I generally keep a large box of spaghetti-like or linguine-like dried Chinese noodles in my pantry for stir-fries or soup. If I'm looking for a noodle with more texture, I might choose sliced or shaved noodles.

WONTON WRAPPERS: Wonton wrappers are ubiquitous and have transcended Chinese cuisine as a utilitarian convenience product. The square wrappers are available in most supermarkets, but if you can get to a Chinese market, you will be able to find different thicknesses. Where a thin wrapper might be used for wonton soup, a thicker wrapper might be used for fried wontons. When in doubt, the label usually designates the best use. You can keep a pack or two in the freezer and defrost as needed. The amount of wrappers per package varies. If you don't use all of them for one recipe, you can seal the leftovers in a freezer bag and freeze for up to several weeks. Defrost overnight in the refrigerator before using.

Tofu

TOFU OR BEAN CURD: Tofu is made from soy milk curds that are pressed into blocks of different firmness: silken, soft, medium, medium firm, firm, extra firm. Tofu is ubiquitous in Chinese cooking, appearing in various forms in every type of dish from appetizers to desserts. For the purposes of the stir-fries and soups in this book, I prefer Chinese-style soft or medium-firm tofu.

TOFU GAN: Also called "spiced tofu," "five-spice tofu," or "pressed tofu," this seasoned tofu becomes extra firm after pressing. It's usually used in cold salads or stir-fries.

Vegetables

BABY BOK CHOY: Also called Shanghai bok choy, these jade-colored cabbages vary in size, with the smallest ones measuring about four inches long. There is also white bok choy, which has a white stalk and dark-green, dimpled leaves. Both types are delicious, though the green variety is likely more familiar to non-Asians.

BAMBOO SHOOTS: In the United States, it's easiest to find bamboo shoots canned. The quality of fresh bamboo shoots is inconsistent unless you live near a vibrant Chinatown. Canned bamboo shoots come in slices, strips, and chunks. Rinse before using.

BEAN SPROUTS: Bean sprouts are versatile and can be stir-fried with other ingredients or used on their own. They add a nice crunch and that telltale sprout flavor.

CHINESE BROCCOLI: Chinese broccoli (*gai lan*) have thick stalks, with a few green leaves at the top. They're commonly served at dim sum restaurants, where the stalks are steamed or blanched and served with oyster sauce. You also can stir-fry Chinese broccoli, if you peel the stalk and slice thinly.

CHINESE CHIVES: You will smell these before you see them because they are pungent. The long stalks are flat. There are green and yellow varieties. Use them in stir-fries and meat fillings.

CHINESE EGGPLANT: Chinese and Japanese eggplants are long and thin. **Prep:** The skin tends to be more tender, so it's not necessary to peel them. Because of the slender shape, it's best to slice them on the bias for stir-frying or steaming.

CHINESE MUSTARD GREENS: Chinese mustard greens (*gai choy*) or mustard cabbage grow in a head. You can buy small or large heads. It's great in stir-fries or pickled. The flavor can be slightly bitter and pungent. **Prep:** There is a large core stem that you have to remove.

NAPA CABBAGE: Also called Chinese cabbage, this is arguably China's national vegetable. The flavor is mild, and its applications are numerous. I keep at least one head of napa cabbage in my refrigerator at all times to use in soups, stir-fries, or dumplings.

PEA SHOOTS: Pea shoots are the leaves of the pea plant. They are fantastic in stir-fries with some minced garlic. Asian markets tend to sell them in large clamshell boxes. **Prep:** Be sure to pick out any tough, chewy stems.

SNOW PEAS: Snow peas are often incorporated into stir-fries for color as well as flavor. They are flatter and less sweet than sugar snap peas.

YU CHOY
WHITE-STEMMED
BOK CHOY
CHINESE BROCCOLI,
OR GAI LAN
CHINESE MUSTARD
GREENS, OR GAI CHOY

SHANGHAI BOK CHOY, OR BABY BOK CHOY
PEA SHOOTS
NAPA CABBAGE, OR CHINESE CABBAGE

WATER SPINACH: A type of green with long, hollow stems and narrow leaves, winter spinach is usually stir-fried with a little garlic. It's commonly called by its Cantonese name *ong choy*.

YAM LEAF: Asian markets sell yam leaves in bags that you can stir-fry. They're tender and spinachlike and have a slightly earthy flavor.

YU CHOY: This is the rapeseed plant from which oil is derived. The Cantonese *yu* or Mandarin *you* stands for "oil." *Choy* is a generic term for "vegetable." Yu choy has long, thin stalks and dark-green leaves. The whole stem can be eaten and is especially delicious in a stir-fry.

A WORD ON WINES

Beer tends to be the go-to pairing for Chinese foods. Pairing wines with a Chinese meal is challenging because there usually are more flavor components in Chinese cooking than any single wine can handle. That said, wines that are crisp, dry or off dry, and have high acidity are good. It's also important to avoid wines that are oaky or are high in tannins. Riesling, Vouvray, Pinot Gris, Chenin Blanc, and sparkling wines are good bets. Lighter red wines, such as a Pinot Noir or a Gamay, can pair with richer and more pungent flavors. When in doubt, go to a reputable wine shop that has knowledgeable staff and ask them to help you choose a wine.

Techniques

The general rule for how to cut vegetables and proteins for Chinese cooking is that the size and shape should be appropriate for the type of cooking. Stir-frying is about quick cooking over high heat, which means that ingredients should be cut into small, similarly sized pieces so that they can cook quickly and evenly. Braises, because they have longer, slower cooking times, can handle larger and tougher cuts of meats. Vegetables are cut into shapes that match the protein as well as the cooking method.

Cutting Meat

CUBE: Chicken is often cut into *ding*—¾-inch or so cubes—for stir-fries.

SLICE: Slices can vary in dimension, but they usually yield the greatest surface area.

SLIVER: In Mandarin, this cut is called *si*, or "thread." It's a great way to make a small amount of meat seem more sumptuous than it is.

Cutting Vegetables

BIAS CUT: Vegetables and aromatics can be sliced thinly on the bias to help create surface area and pretty visuals.

DICE: Dice can range from small to large, depending on the type of vegetable and preparation.

MINCE: Mincing is usually used for aromatics, such as garlic and ginger. Meats also can be minced by chopping.

ROLL CUT: A roll cut is great for root vegetables or squash to create surface area for flavor and texture.

SLIVER: Fine, threadlike cuts of aromatics and vegetables, slivers are commonly used for garnishes or for hard vegetables, such as carrots, so that they cook more quickly.

SLICE: Slices yield thinly cut rounds of ginger, carrots, cucumber, and the like.

DICE
ROLL CUT
SLICE
BIAS CUT
MINCE
DICE
SLIVER

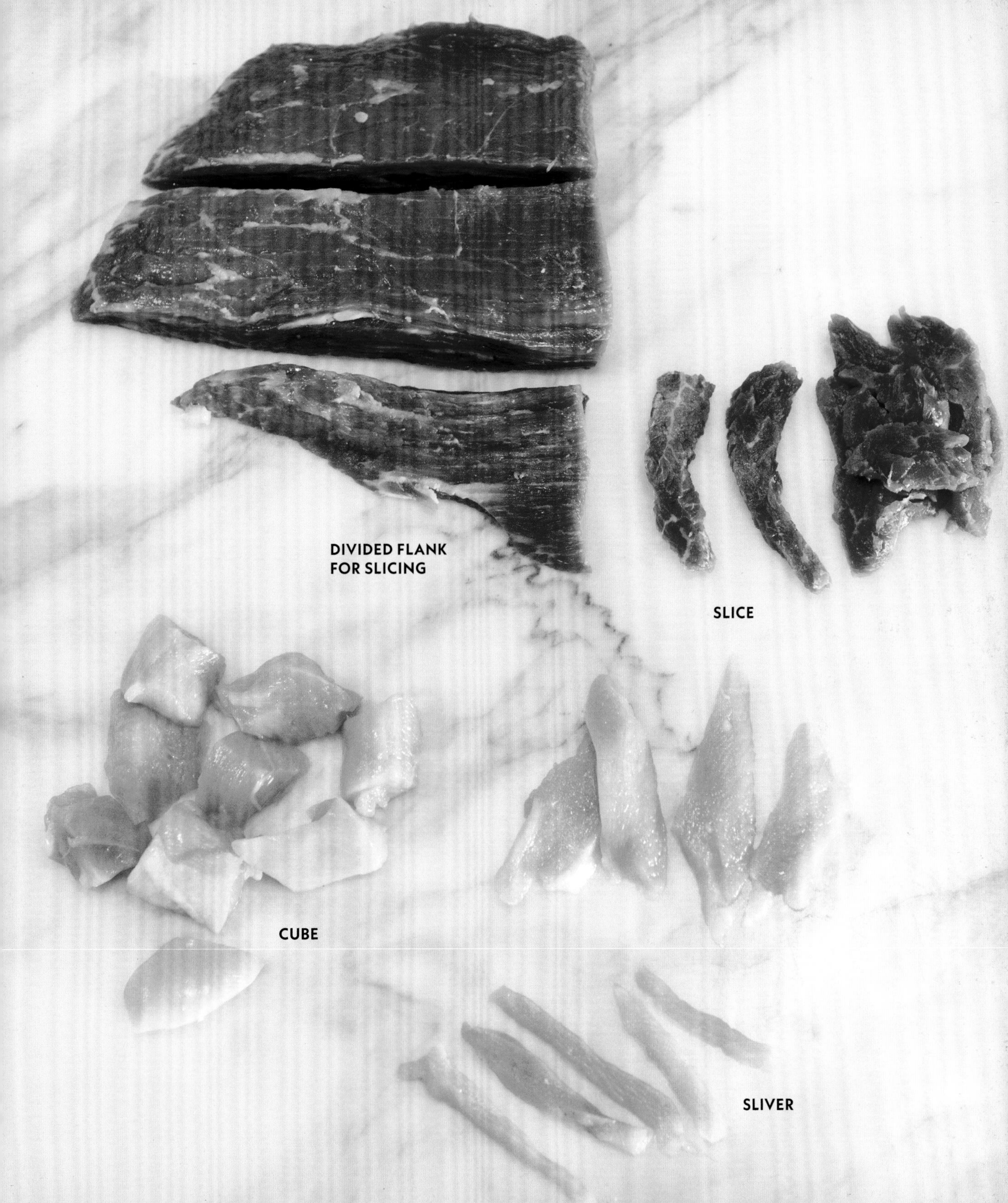
DIVIDED FLANK
FOR SLICING
SLICE
CUBE
SLIVER

Cooking Methods

FRYING: Deep or shallow frying is often used as an intermediary step to add a layer of texture to a dish, such as with Orange Beef (page 159) or Three-Cup Chicken (page 152). Frying is also used for making crispy appetizers, such as spring rolls or fried wontons.

RED BRAISING: Red braising is a common method for simmering ingredients in a soy-sauce-based liquid. The timing of the braise is shorter for delicate proteins, such as a whole fish, and longer for meats, such as beef shank. The result is a rich, savory dish.

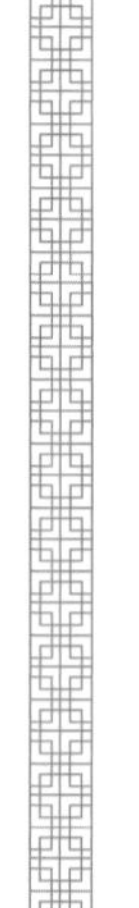

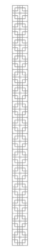

PREP WORK

Before you get started, read through the recipe. Before you cook, cut and measure all the ingredients. When it's time to apply heat, especially for stir-frying, you have to be able to move quickly. You will not have time to find and measure ingredients when the total cooking time is just a few minutes. The French call this prep work *mise en place*, or "put everything in place."

STIR-FRYING: Stir-frying is likely the most-used Chinese cooking technique. I could go a week or two without steaming or braising, but I wouldn't survive without being able to stir-fry. Here is the basic protocol for stir-frying.

1. Cut all the ingredients into appropriate, similarly sized pieces.
2. Season the protein.
3. Preheat the wok over high heat until wisps of smoke rise from the surface.
4. Parcook the protein: Add oil and heat for a few seconds until the oil shimmers. Add the protein and, using the wok spatula, stir-fry the protein to sear the outside and begin to cook it through. Transfer the protein to a bowl and set aside.
5. Rinse and dry the wok.
6. Return the wok to high heat. (Since the wok is already warm, it won't need as much time to preheat.) Add oil and immediately add aromatics, such as green onions, garlic, and ginger. Stir-fry for a few seconds to release the aromas.
7. Add the vegetables and stir-fry to combine.
8. Add the protein and stir-fry to combine.
9. Add the sauce and stir-fry to combine.
10. Finish with a drizzle of sesame oil and serve.
11. Wash the wok with warm water and a gentle sponge, but no soap. Dry thoroughly and store.

STEAMING: From the Western perspective, steaming often gets negatively associated with "bland" or "healthy" foods. From the Chinese perspective, steaming is an art. The moist-heat cooking transforms yeasted doughs into airy buns, seafoods into intensified versions of themselves, meats into tender morsels of savoriness, and so on. While there are different styles of steamers (see page 49), the most traditional option is the stackable bamboo steamer.

HOW TO SET UP A BAMBOO STEAMER:

- 4- to 5-quart Dutch oven
- 1 (11-inch) steaming ring
- 1 (10-inch) bamboo steamer
- Round perforated parchment steamer liners

Fill a 4- to 5-quart Dutch oven, or equivalent pan, with 3 quarts water. Bring the water to a boil over high heat. Line the steamer basket with parchment and place the food in the basket. Place the steaming ring on the rim of the Dutch oven and set the steamer basket and lid on the ringer. Steam over high heat, as directed. Be sure to check the water level from time to time to make sure the pot doesn't dry up. All of the components of the bamboo steamer and accessories are available online through Amazon.com or Wokshop.com.

Equipment

My kitchen is integrated when it comes to frequently used tools. While I stir-fry exclusively in a wok, I don't use the wok for everything. I'm more likely to braise in a Dutch oven, deep-fry in the tabletop fryer, and set my bamboo steamer over one of my stainless-steel saucepots. I own two cleavers, but I rarely use them—except for when I need to chop chicken wings in half for Three-Cup Chicken (page 152). I prefer my 8-inch chef's knife or 5½-inch santoku because they're more lightweight and easier for me to handle.

CANNING JARS: I like to store sauces, oils, spices, and other shelf-stable ingredients in canning jars. It's also good to have jars on hand if you plan on making Pickled Chinese Mustard Greens (page 157).

CHOPSTICKS: Chopsticks can be used for a range of tasks in the kitchen, including beating eggs, mixing fillings for dumplings, filling dumplings, frying foods, and placing or arranging foods on plates. Everyday bamboo chopsticks are great, or you can buy cooking chopsticks, which are about 15 inches long. The extra length makes it easier to handle ingredients that are still in the active stages of cooking.

CLEAVER: You can buy a Chinese cleaver at any Asian market. They're widely available and not too expensive. The beauty of the cleaver is that you can use it for cutting fine threads of vegetables, chopping through bone, and scooping up ingredients, like you would with a bench scraper.

FAT SKIMMER: This tool helps to skim fat and scum off of broths and braises.

FINE-MESH SIEVES: I keep assorted sizes of fine-mesh sieves for straining broths or sauces that contain loose aromatics.

METAL WORK BOWLS: I keep a stack of lightweight, stainless-steel work bowls in several sizes. They're durable, convenient, and essential for containing all the prepped ingredients.

RICE COOKER: Rice cookers range from the conventional one-button models that get the job done to high-end computerized cookers that are programmable and adjust the soaking, cooking, and steaming times according to the type of rice. The cost can be anywhere from twenty to five hundred dollars. When I was single, a

3- or 6-cup, no-frills cooker was just fine. With a family, a 10-cup rice cooker makes more sense. If you spend about sixty or seventy dollars, you get a decent cooker that can accommodate several varieties of rice and offers the option to have a softer or harder texture. If you are a rice aficionado and you're willing to drop a few hundred bucks, you can get a cooker that has fuzzy logic technology, which, among many features, can sense if the rice is cooking too quickly and adjust the heat as necessary.

ROLLING PIN: Chinese rolling pins resemble wooden dowels and aren't tapered. They're about twelve inches in length and just under one inch in diameter. Asian markets sell these for less than two dollars each. If you do get a wooden dowel from the hardware store, be sure to get one that has about a 3/4-inch diameter with a smooth surface.

SAUCE DISHES: Small ceramic dip bowls are not only great for serving dipping sauces but also perfect for holding spices, minced garlic or ginger, and other aromatics. You can line the dishes up in the order that you're adding the particular ingredient, which helps to keep you organized. Asian markets usually have the widest selection of shapes and designs.

STEAMER: Steamers are available in bamboo, stainless steel, and aluminum. You can find an assortment of dedicated steamer pots at any Asian market. All work well. Or you can get, say, a 3-piece, 10-inch bamboo steamer set plus an 11-inch steaming ring that will allow you to convert a Dutch oven or stockpot into a steamer system. I have several steamers, but my two go-to steamers are a 10-inch bamboo steamer and a 16-inch aluminum steamer. I use the bamboo to steam dumplings. The bamboo lid prevents condensation from dripping on the dumplings. I use the aluminum steamer for whole duck or whole fish. While my wok and rice cooker both can be used as steamers, I find it more convenient to use dedicated steamers.

STEAMER PAPER: You can get precut, perforated parchment circles to line your steamer. Food-safe synthetic-cotton steamer sheets are also available at some Chinese markets. This prevents food from sticking.

STRAINER/SPIDER: A spider is useful for straining and lifting foods out of hot oil or boiling water.

WOK: If I were to choose one piece of required equipment to buy, it would be a wok. By definition, stir-frying is the cooking method associated with a wok. The bowl

WOK SPATULA

WOK LADLE

DOUGH MIXER

SPIDER/STRAINER

FINE-
MESH
SIEVE

CHEF'S KNIFE

MEAT CLEAVER

ROLLING PIN
BAMBOO
STEAMER
FAT SKIMMER
STEAMER PAPER
ALL-PURPOSE
CLEAVER

HOW TO SEASON AND MAINTAIN YOUR WOK

If it's brand new, scrub it with soap and hot tap water to rid the surface of the factory finish. Dry with a towel. Set the wok on the stove over high heat. The heat helps to dry the wok completely. When the wok is really hot, there will be tiny wisps of smoke. Next, coat the wok with oil: Starting from about 2 inches below the rim, slowly and in a swirling motion pour 3 tablespoons of vegetable oil down the side of the wok. Reduce the heat to low. Add one bunch of green onions that have been cut into 3-inch segments and ½ cup sliced ginger rounds (¼ inch thick; no need to peel). It will sizzle a bit. Now, using a spatula, stir and toss the onions and ginger together. Then, using the combination like a sponge, push it up and down the sides of the wok to help coat the surface with oil. Do this for 2 to 3 minutes. Remove the wok from the heat and discard the onions and ginger. Wipe the wok with a wad of paper towels to absorb any excess oil. Let it cool. The wok is now ready to go. Over time, especially if you use the wok to fry, the oil will help to develop the patina in the wok.

Treat your wok like a cast-iron pan. Rinse it immediately in warm water after use and give it a gentle scrub with a sponge, but don't use soap, as it can strip off the patina. Dry the wok thoroughly to prevent rusting. With a new wok, I will put it back on the heat for about 1 minute to dry. I don't bother with that step now that my main wok is well seasoned. If you do get some rust, scrub it with a steel scrubber and then reseason.

shape of a traditional round-bottom wok concentrates the high heat in the center and creates a "cool" zone on the sides. The cool zone is useful when you are searing individual ingredients in quick succession before stir-frying them together. After you're done searing the ingredient, you use your wok spatula to scoot it up the side to hold until you're ready to mix it together with the other ingredients. For most home cooks, a 12- or 14-inch carbon steel round- or flat-bottom wok will suffice. You can select your choice of handle configuration, though I'd recommend a wok with a wooden side handle. If you have a high-powered gas stove, you may want to consider getting a wok with metal loop handles instead of wood, which will burn. Do not spend more than twenty to forty dollars. Carbon steel heats—and cools—quickly and is relatively lightweight.

If you have a gas stove, you can get a traditional round-bottom wok with a wok ring, which is a stand that holds the wok above the burner. Some stove manufacturers have custom wok rings, so check with the maker of your stove before spending money on a generic wok ring. If you have an electric or induction stove, get a flat-bottom wok to ensure full contact with the heat source. A flat-bottom wok also works on a gas stove, but a round-bottom wok is more traditional.

Nonstick and stainless-steel woks aren't ideal. Nonstick surfaces don't support high-heat cooking and prevent you from getting a proper sear. Stainless-steel

MR. CEN WOKS

My friend Grace Young, who has written several cookbooks on Chinese cooking, discovered the Cen brothers' hand-hammered woks on a trip to Shanghai in 2000. Through her storytelling, these gorgeous woks gained international fame and inspired many people to go on pilgrimages to secure their own Cen wok. In Grace's stories about the Cen brothers, she explains that what makes the hand-hammered woks special is that the pounding reinforces the structure of the carbon steel and the resulting "dimples" help to distribute the heat more evenly. The Cen woks also develop a perfectly even and dark patina that contributes to the telltale wok flavor and a naturally nonstick surface. I didn't get a chance to visit the Cen brothers before their stall was forced to shut down by developers. But I'm fortunate to have friends who happened to be visiting Shanghai—before the Cens shut down—and were willing to seek out the shop and bring back woks for me. I now have two Cen woks that I hope to pass on to my children. These handcrafted woks cost about twenty US dollars each. I mention this to emphasize that a quality wok, whether made by an artisan in Shanghai or a large factory in Hong Kong, should not cost you more than twenty to forty dollars. While the Cen brothers may not be in business any longer, there are, perhaps, other artisans who have yet to be discovered and revered.

woks, especially name-brand versions, tend to be expensive and too heavy, and they aren't naturally nonstick like a well-seasoned wok. Cast-iron woks are available, but they can be quite heavy, and, because they retain heat so well, it's easy to overcook food. A carbon-steel wok is your best bet.

Even if you have the right wok for the right type of stove, the variable that causes the most hiccups is the power of the heat. A crappy old electric stove in an old apartment simply isn't going to provide the same kind of heat output as a high-end gas stove. Preheating the wok and not overcrowding the ingredients—and relying on cooking in smaller batches—will be essential to overcoming a weak stove. Don't be discouraged, though; be resourceful and adaptable. A great source for woks is Wokshop.com.

WOK LADLE: Many Chinese cooks, especially restaurant chefs, use the wok ladle to cook because the bowl of the ladle can be used to measure or scoop liquids, as well as perform all the usual stir-fry functions. It has a straight handle similar to the wok spatula. Whichever wok spatula you select, buy a matching or similar wok ladle.

WOK SPATULA: Chinese wok spatulas have a long handle and are usually made from stainless steel with a wooden or plastic handle at the end. The blade end is slightly rounded to match the curve of the round-bottomed wok. This is used to stir, shovel, and toss ingredients in the wok. I prefer stainless steel so I don't have to worry about melting any plastic in hot oil. I suggest getting a 14- or 16-inch wok spatula and spending no more than ten dollars.

A WORD ON ETIQUETTE

Dining etiquette is less about which utensil to use—chopsticks, of course—and more about the hierarchy of the people around the table. The eldest person is the most revered, as are guests, especially if they have traveled from afar. Since meals are typically served family style, it means the host will take care of serving the most senior person or the guest first. The guest may defer, then the host will fuss and insist, and finally the guest will accept and profess an abundance of appreciation. If dinner is at a restaurant, this routine will continue with each course until the bill arrives. That's when it becomes a competition to see who can grab the check first. The other person usually tries to steal the bill, and so it goes until the "winner" shoves the bill and the money into the hand of the cashier. This is normal, and no one bats an eyelash when they witness such a duel in public. In general, it is polite to serve your neighbor before serving yourself. When you serve your neighbor, you dish out generous portions. When you serve yourself, you take a more modest amount. As a guest, you follow the host's lead, deferring to his or her judgment when it comes to the menu. This is the polar opposite of how dinner happens in the West, where each person has an individual meal or, if the meal is family style, each person piles the food on his or her own plate without regard to others.

Speaking of chopsticks, it's important to note some dos and don'ts:

- Don't use chopsticks as drumsticks. Period.
- Don't stab food with chopsticks. Do use a spoon to help you pick up food, if you are having trouble picking up slippery foods, such as noodles.
- Chopsticks are not meant to be held like a knife and fork to break apart food. Do ask for a knife.
- Don't use your chopsticks to push or pull a dish of food around on the table. Do ask the person closest to the dish to pass it to you.
- Don't use your personal chopsticks to serve food to others or yourself. Do use the serving spoon or serving chopsticks.
- Don't cross your chopsticks. It symbolizes death.
- Don't shove the chopsticks in your food or rice when resting between bites or courses. It symbolizes death. Do place your chopsticks flat on the table next to your plate or on the chopstick rest.
- Don't use your chopsticks to gesture or point.

包子、餃子，麵點

Dumplings

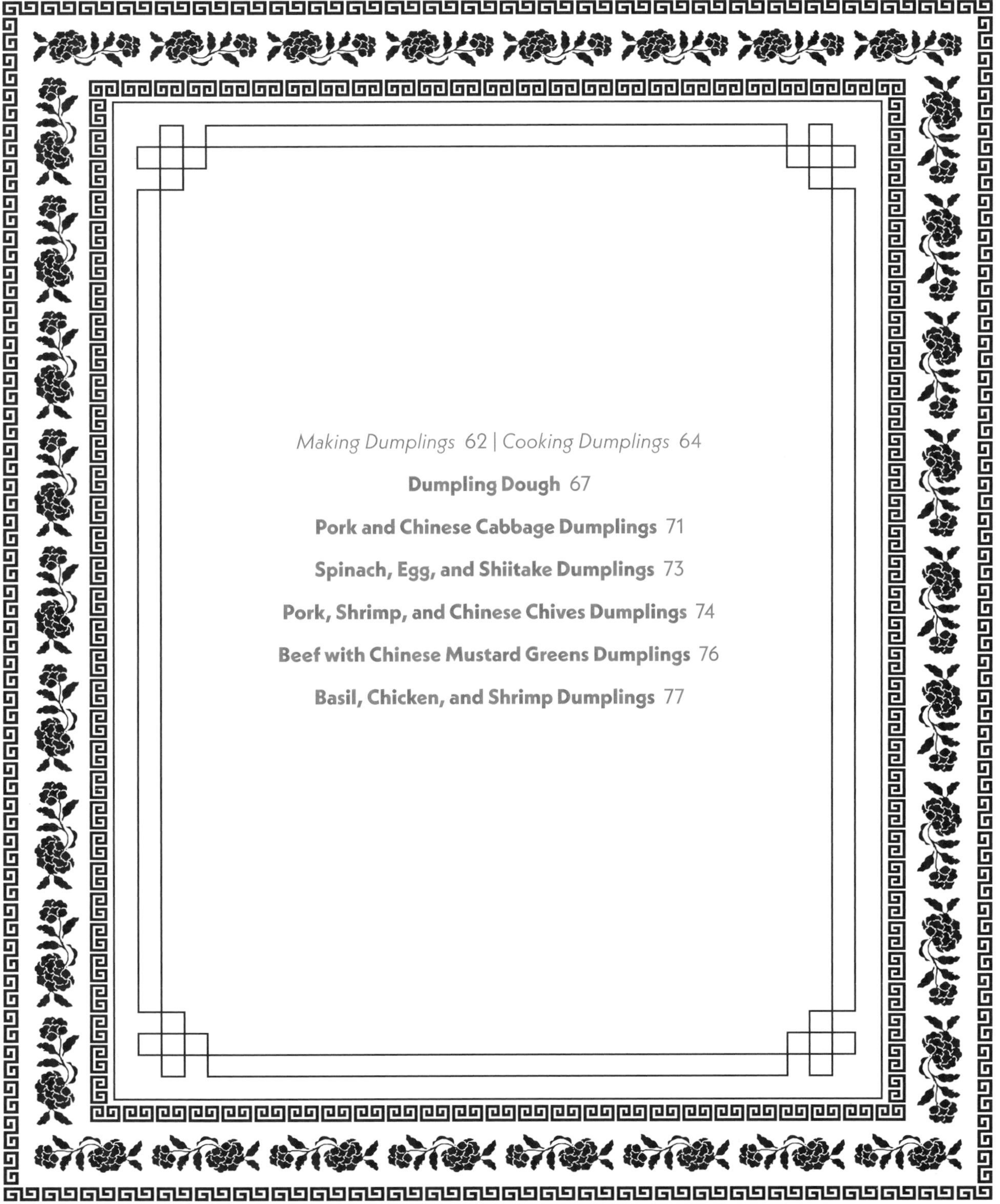

Dumplings, whether steamed, boiled, or panfried, are a perfect food when it comes to the potential combinations of flavors and textures. One dough can carry you through any number of fillings and your favorite cooking method. I prefer my Spinach, Egg, and Shiitake Dumplings steamed. I like the traditional Pork and Chinese Cabbage Dumplings boiled or panfried. They're best hot, but there have been plenty of times when I've eaten dumplings cold out of the refrigerator. They're filling and portable, and assembling them is typically a communal activity that brings friends and families together. My earliest memory of dumpling making as an act of community is when my father was studying for his master's degree in journalism and we were living in student housing for families. I was probably five or six years old at the time. It was a tiny apartment, but my parents moved the dinner table into the middle of the living room, and their friends gathered around to share dumpling-making duties. We didn't have a proper dowel-style Chinese rolling pin, so my father somehow—I don't recall his having a saw—cut off the end of our wooden broom handle. It was aqua blue and the perfect diameter. Broom handles nowadays are mostly plastic or aluminum, or have molded grips. It'd be pretty hard to cut a rolling pin out of that.

I learned how to make dumplings at my mother's side. She would prepare the dough and roll out the wrappers. I would fill the dumplings and pinch them closed. When I was about sixteen or so, my father put me to test and said I had to demonstrate I could make dumplings from beginning to end all on my own. "How are you going to find a husband if you can't make dumplings?" he said to me once. Even though I bristled at the thought of being a demure wife, it was a prescient statement: my husband fell for my strong sense of self, but when he bragged about me to his friends, he always talked about my pot stickers. For any gathering we hosted in our little apartment, he insisted that I make pot stickers, regardless of the menu. Even now, all these years later, he asks me if I'm going to make dumplings for dinner parties, especially when his side of the family comes over.

I have been on a mission for as long as I have been a food writer to convert dumpling eaters into dumpling makers, especially when it comes to the panfried dumplings that everyone knows as pot stickers. When I was fresh out of college and working at the *Denver Post* as a copyeditor on the night shift, my colleagues sometimes ordered Chinese takeout for dinner. They all fawned over the pot stickers, but I would look at the lifeless, greasy dumplings with mild contempt, mumbling to myself about how they tasted like shortcuts: cheap ingredients and poorly

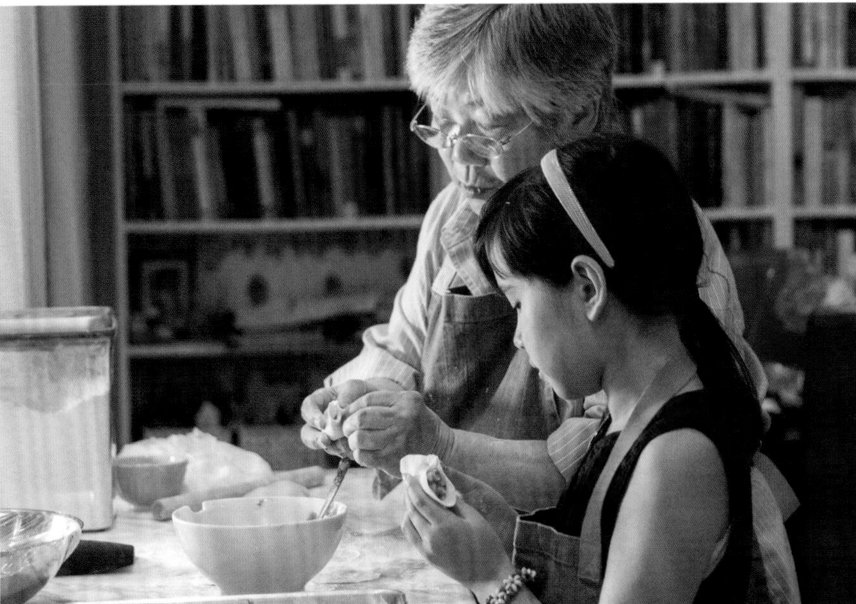

formed crust. The crispy crust is why these dumplings are called pot stickers, after all. One of my copy desk friends, undoubtedly tired of hearing me grumble, offered to introduce me to her famous pierogies if I would make my pot stickers for her. I willingly accepted, and thus began two decades of pot sticker proselytizing.

After three years in Denver, I moved to Seattle to serve as the food writer for the *Seattle Post-Intelligencer*. That's when my reputation became bound with pot stickers. I'd make them for friends and colleagues. I wrote about them and demonstrated them at various culinary events. Then I took the show on the road, so to speak, as a guest chef on a cruise to China. I remember traipsing around Shanghai in search of enough Chinese rolling pins to give to my students on the ship and finally finding them in bulk at, of all places, Carrefour, a French-owned supermarket chain. My pot stickers experienced their fifteen minutes of fame in a segment on Anthony Bourdain's Travel Channel show *No Reservations*. He remembered my pot stickers from our previous encounter in Seattle and wanted to shoot a segment where he would come to my house for a pot sticker lesson. These days, I teach monthly classes on Chinese home cooking, and the pot sticker and soup dumpling classes always sell out far in advance.

Making Dumplings

Dumpling Dough (page 67) is versatile and is used regardless of the filling or the cooking method. Make the dough, make one or more of the fillings (see pages 71 to 77), and proceed to fill and fold the dumplings, per the instructions below. You then can decide which cooking method you want to follow (see Cooking Dumplings, page 64). You could boil and panfry, for example, or panfry all the dumplings. It's up to you. Finally, you can serve them with one or more dipping sauces (see pages 72 and 75).

Filling Dumplings

Roll out about 6 wrappers at a time per Dumpling Dough instructions (page 67). Fill each wrapper with about 1 heaping teaspoon of your filling of choice.

Folding Dumplings

The simplest way to seal a dumpling is to fold the wrapper over the filling into a half-moon shape. Match the edges together and press as if you were sealing an envelope. There is no need to dab homemade wrappers with water. There is enough moisture in the dough that the edges will seal when pressed. Holding the sealed edge of the dumpling between your fingers, set it on its spine and gently wiggle it as you are pushing down so that the dumpling will stand up. Place the completed dumpling on a baking sheet dusted with flour or lined with parchment paper. Repeat with the remaining dumplings.

To learn how to pleat the dumplings, see the step-by-step photos (opposite page).

Storing Dumplings

Once you have made all the dumplings, you can cook them immediately or freeze them. If you freeze them, place the baking sheet of dumplings in the freezer for about 30 minutes to harden enough so they don't stick together. Then, transfer the dumplings to a ziplock bag and place them in the freezer to store for up to two or three weeks. You can cook them from frozen. Do not defrost or you will get a gooey mess. If you are cooking the dumplings immediately, proceed to any of the dumpling recipes in this chapter, and use the cooking methods found in Cooking Dumplings (page 64).

Cooking Dumplings

You can use any combination of filling and cooking method for the dumplings. It all depends on what you crave.

My father loved to eat dumplings cooked every way. He was always the taste tester to see if the dumplings were cooked through. When boiling dumplings, my mom would scoop one dumpling out of the bubbling water, hand it to my father, and ask him, "Is it done?" He'd carefully take a bite of the dumpling and proclaim, "Yes, it's done." In the restaurant, we had this giant, thirty-inch commercial wok that easily accommodated the entire batch of dumplings at one time.

Steamed dumplings have the benefit of not getting waterlogged like the boiled dumplings. You can use a bamboo or metal steamer lined with blanched Chinese cabbage leaves or liners made of perforated parchment paper, which you can buy online or at Asian markets. You also can cut your own parchment circles and use a hole puncher or a skewer to make enough holes in the paper to let steam through.

Panfried dumplings, or pot stickers, seem to be a great equalizer. I don't think I've met a person who doesn't like pot stickers. Even burned pot stickers taste good—just ask my brother, who ate a plate of pot stickers I accidentally burned while attending to another matter. Even though I hid the burnt ones, my brother found them and ate them anyway. When we have extended family over for dinner, there never seems to be enough pot (*guo*) stickers (*tie*) to go around. Being able to make big batches of pot stickers is the reason I own a large nonstick skillet. The nonstick surface browns well and releases the dumplings more consistently. You also can use a cast-iron pan.

To Boil Dumplings

In a large soup pot or stockpot over high heat, bring 4 quarts of water to a boil. Carefully add about half of the prepared dumplings, or only as many as your pot can accommodate without crowding. Return to a boil and then cook the dumplings for 4½ to 5 minutes. If you are cooking frozen dumplings, boil them for 1 to 2 minutes more. Keep an eye on the water as it may bubble over, and adjust the heat as necessary. The dumplings are done when they puff up. Remove the pot from the heat. Using a large slotted spoon or handled strainer, transfer the dumplings to a serving plate.

To Steam Dumplings

Set up the steamer (see page 47). Line a steamer basket with steamer paper or perforated parchment paper, and place the prepared dumplings in a single layer in the basket, leaving about 1 inch between dumplings. Place the steamer basket on top of the pot, and steam, covered, for 8 to 10 minutes, or until the wrappers puff up. The cooking time will depend on the filling; meat fillings take longer. If you are cooking frozen dumplings, steam them for 1 to 2 minutes more.

To Panfry Dumplings (Pot Stickers)

Preheat an 8- or 9-inch nonstick skillet over medium heat for about 1 minute. (If you have a bigger or smaller skillet, that's fine. Adjust the oil amount as needed.) Avoid high heat, which can cause the nonstick coating to deteriorate. Add enough vegetable oil to generously coat the entire surface of the pan and create a slight pool of oil (about 1/8 inch deep). This may seem like a lot of oil, but it will help you create that telltale crispy pot sticker crust.

Carefully arrange the dumplings in a single layer in the skillet, flat side down. Add 1/2 cup water to the skillet and cover immediately. Cook for 7 to 9 minutes, or until the water has evaporated and the bottoms of the dumplings have reached a golden brown. The cooking time may vary slightly depending on your stove. Frozen dumplings may need 1 minute more to cook. Adjust the heat as needed.

If you have leftover dumplings, store them in the refrigerator and eat within a couple of days. To reheat, place them in a lightly oiled pan over medium-low heat and let the filling come to temperature. This will refresh the crispiness of the crust. Or you can eat them cold, as I sometimes do.

PANFRY VARIATION

To make pot sticker lace: The best part of the pot sticker is the crispy crust. Some restaurants add starch water to the pan, which crisps up to create a lacy sheet of crust surrounding the pot stickers. In a small bowl, place 1 tablespoon plus 1½ teaspoons cornstarch to ½ cup water and mix to combine. Instead of water, add this mixture to the pan. It will result in a lacy crust. Be sure to flip the dumplings over on a plate so that the beautiful crust is facing up.

A NOTE ON DUMPLING VERNACULAR

In the Chinese language, each type of dumpling or bun has its own name that denotes the type of wrapper, filling, folding technique, and cooking method. These don't always translate concisely into English. For example, *xiao long tang bao* literally means "little steamer basket soup dumpling." In English, we call them soup dumplings or, if we refer to the transliteration, we say *xiao long bao* or XLB. This isn't precise, however. In Chinese, we distinguish *xiao long bao* and *xiao long* tang *bao*, because there are versions that don't have soup in them and *tang* (sounds like "tahng," not Tang the orange drink) indicates the kind that contains soup. Confusion also surrounds the term "pot stickers," which has become so ubiquitous in English that people mistakenly use it as a generic term for these crescent-shaped, meat-filled dumplings. In Chinese, we use *jiao zi* as the general term. If we boil them, we use *shui jiao*, or "water dumpling." Steamed dumplings are *zheng jiao* and panfried pot stickers are *guo tie*. Dialectical differences in transliterations increase the level of difficulty. Case in point: The Cantonese term for shrimp (*har*) dumplings (*gow*) in wheat starch wrappers is *har gow*. The Mandarin term is *xia jiao*. The Cantonese *siu mai* or *shumai* is the Mandarin *shao mai*. You know these dumplings, of course, from visits to Cantonese dim sum (or *dian xin* in Mandarin) restaurants. Navigating these terms is, indeed, challenging—this is why you see picture menus in Chinese restaurants. Assume that there is usually something lost in translation and, when in doubt, ask.

和麵

Dumpling Dough

MAKES ABOUT 1 POUND DOUGH (FOR ABOUT 48 DUMPLINGS)

2½ cups unbleached all-purpose flour, plus more for dusting

¾ cup plus 1 tablespoon warm water (about 105 to 110 degrees F)

All-purpose flour and water. It really doesn't get more straightforward than that. What takes practice is using your eyes and sense of touch to determine just how thirsty the flour is on a given day, because the moisture content of the flour and the humidity in the air both can affect how the dough comes together. I tell you this so that you know you need to pay attention, but I don't want you to stress about these factors. If the dough feels too sticky, then a little more flour will bring the dough back into balance. The recipe calls for warm water because flour absorbs warm water more easily and it creates a more supple texture. This dough can be used for dumplings, Green Onion Pancakes (page 90), or Home-Style Hand-Cut Noodles (page 129). You will need a Chinese rolling pin. This recipe yields enough dumplings that you can freeze extras to serve another time.

▪ Put the flour in a large bowl. Add all of the water. Using a rubber spatula, a wooden spoon, a pair of chopsticks, or your fingers, stir the water and flour together until a shaggy ball of dough starts to form. Now, use your hands to start kneading the dough and incorporating any remaining flour. The dough should feel slightly tacky but not damp. It should not stick to your fingers.

▪ Dust your work surface with flour. Remove the dough from the bowl and knead for about 2 minutes. It should feel smooth. Cover the dough with a damp towel or plastic wrap and let it rest on the counter for a minimum of 20 minutes. (While it doesn't need much longer than that, it won't hurt the dough if it happens to rest longer.)

▪ Alternatively, you can use a stand mixer to form the dough. Add the flour to the bowl of the stand mixer, and add the water gradually while running the dough hook at medium-low speed. Once the dough comes together, knead for about 2 minutes. Cover the dough and let it rest for 20 minutes. (This dough will hold for several hours at room temperature. It will get stickier, so you will have to knead in about 1 to 2 tablespoons of flour to refresh it. It's best to make this dough the same day you want to use it.)

▪ Once rested, divide the dough in half. On a surface lightly dusted with flour, roll each half into a rope that's about ¾ inch in diameter and about 18 inches in length. Using a knife or a bench scraper, cut each rope into pieces that are about ¾ inch thick. Each piece should weigh about 9 or 10 grams (see note, page 69).

→

- Roll each piece of dough into a small ball and then flatten it between your palms to create a disc that resembles a wafer cookie. Press your thumb gently into the dough to create a small indentation. Position your rolling pin between you and the base of the wafer of dough. Dust lightly with flour as needed. Roll the pin forward across the dough and back. You do not need to lift the rolling pin. Turn the dough 90 degrees and repeat the forward-and-back rolling. Turn the dough 90 degrees again and repeat the rolling. This forms the beginnings of a circle.

- Repeat this for the second revolution, but, for subsequent turns, roll the pin only halfway up. For the third revolution, roll the pin only a third of the way up. The idea is to leave the center of the circle just slightly thicker than the outer edges. The wrapper should end up being a circle about 3¼ inches in diameter. Don't worry if the circle isn't perfect; it only needs to be roundish. If it looks like an oval, then round it out. If it's lopsided beyond repair, then bunch up the dough into a ball and start again. Unless you have an assembly line of friends or family helping you, roll out about six wrappers at a time. If you roll out too many, they start to stick to each other and the edges will dry out, which makes it harder to seal.

NOTE: These dimensions are meant as a guideline. You could make these larger, if you'd like. You would end up with fewer dumplings and each would require more filling. The key is to keep the size consistent, so the dumplings cook consistently. I wouldn't make these smaller, however, because it makes it more challenging to fold the dumplings, especially if you have big hands or you are a beginner.

If you don't have time to make your own wrappers, you can use store-bought dumpling or gyoza wrappers. There are many brands available, and most stores these days sell at least one type of dumpling wrapper. At Chinese markets, you can usually find thin, medium, and thick dumpling wrappers. The thicker ones are better for pot stickers, because they won't tear as easily. Dab water on the edges to help seal.

猪肉白菜餡

Pork and Chinese Cabbage Dumplings

MAKES ABOUT 45 TO 50 DUMPLINGS

1 batch Dumpling Dough (page 67)

Soy-Ginger Dipping Sauce (recipe follows), for serving

For the filling:

1 pound ground pork

2½ cups loosely packed, finely chopped Chinese cabbage

2 tablespoons soy sauce

1 stalk green onion, finely chopped

1 teaspoon minced ginger

1 teaspoon sesame oil

¼ teaspoon white pepper powder

Pork and Chinese cabbage make the classic dumpling filling. I recommend using the best ground pork you can find. I buy ground Kurobuta pork. Kurobuta is the Japanese name for the Berkshire breed of pig. It's a high-quality pork that has plenty of marbling, which gives the filling great flavor. You also can buy ground pork from your favorite local farmer. If you have access only to what is available at your nearest supermarket, it's totally fine. This recipe will work. What I suggest is to buy unseasoned bulk sausage instead of the regular ground pork, which tends to be too lean, making the flavor flat after it's cooked. The other option, if you have a meat grinder, is to grind some pork butt for the filling. Chinese cabbage, also called napa cabbage, is widely available. The filling can be made up to a day ahead.

- Make the dough according to the recipe. While the dough is resting, make the Soy-Ginger Dipping Sauce and set aside.
- To make the filling, in a medium bowl, combine the pork, cabbage, soy sauce, onions, ginger, oil, and pepper, and mix well. Set the filling aside.
- Fill the wrappers with the prepared filling (see Making Dumplings, page 62).
- Boil, steam, or panfry the dumplings (see Cooking Dumplings, page 64), and serve with the dipping sauce.

→

Soy-Ginger Dipping Sauce

MAKES ABOUT ½ CUP

⅓ cup soy sauce

2 tablespoons rice vinegar

1 stalk green onion, finely chopped

2 large cloves garlic, finely chopped or crushed

1 tablespoon chopped fresh cilantro

1 teaspoon minced fresh ginger

1 teaspoon chili sauce (optional)

People tell me that they could drink this sauce. In fact, I've caught my son sneaking sips of this sauce even before the pot stickers were ready. It hits all the right spots on your palate with its salty, vinegary, pungent flavors. You can add more or less of any given ingredient. Instead of rice vinegar, you could use Chinese black vinegar or balsamic vinegar.

▪ In a small bowl, combine the soy sauce, vinegar, onions, garlic, cilantro, ginger, and chili sauce. Set aside on the counter for at least 30 minutes, if possible, to let the flavors meld together. The longer the mixture rests, the more intense the flavor becomes. You can store the dipping sauce in a sealed container in the refrigerator for up to 1 week.

雞蛋、菠菜冬菇餡

Spinach, Egg, and Shiitake Dumplings

MAKES ABOUT 45 TO 50 DUMPLINGS

1 batch Dumpling Dough (page 67) or store-bought dumpling wrappers

Soy-Ginger Dipping Sauce (page 72), for serving

For the filling:

2 tablespoons vegetable oil, divided

2 large eggs, beaten

2 stalks green onions, finely chopped

2 cloves garlic, minced

10 ounces fresh baby spinach (about 8 cups packed), roughly chopped

1 tablespoon water

1 cup grated carrots (from about 2 medium carrots)

6 medium dried shiitake mushrooms, soaked in warm water to reconstitute, finely diced (about ½ cup)

1 small bundle bean thread noodles, soaked in warm water to reconstitute, roughly chopped (about 1 cup)

2 tablespoons soy sauce

Kosher salt

½ teaspoon sesame oil

I love this filling so much that I can eat a bowl of it on its own. The recipe calls for fresh baby spinach, but you can use frozen chopped spinach. Once defrosted, be sure to squeeze out the liquid before combining with the other ingredients. If you plan on steaming the dumplings, the store-bought dumpling wrappers actually work quite well with this filling.

■ Make the dough according to the recipe. While the dough is resting, make the Soy-Ginger Dipping Sauce and set aside.

■ To make the filling, preheat a wok over medium-high heat for about 1 minute. Add 1 tablespoon of the vegetable oil and heat for about 5 seconds, or until it starts to shimmer. Add the eggs, gently scramble them, and cook until the curds are medium hard. You don't want the eggs too soft or rubbery. Remove the wok from the heat, transfer the eggs to a medium bowl, and set aside. Rinse the wok and dry it completely.

■ Return the wok to the stove and preheat over high heat for 10 seconds. Add the remaining 1 tablespoon vegetable oil, and immediately add the onions and garlic. Stir vigorously for 30 seconds to allow the aromatics to release into the oil. Add the spinach and the water, and stir and toss for about 30 seconds to cook down the spinach. Add the eggs, carrots, and mushrooms, and stir well to combine. Add the bean thread, stir, and reduce the heat to low. Add soy sauce and stir to combine. If you are not attentive, the bean thread may stick to the wok. Stir continuously and adjust the heat if necessary. Add salt to taste, if needed. Add the sesame oil. Stir once again, then remove the wok from the heat and transfer the filling to a medium heatproof bowl. Spread the filling up along the sides of the bowl to help it cool. Set the filling aside.

■ Make the dumpling dough according to the recipe, and fill the wrappers with the prepared filling (see Making Dumplings, page 62).

■ Boil, steam, or panfry the dumplings (see Cooking Dumplings, page 64), and serve with the dipping sauce.

猪肉鲜蝦韭菜餡

Pork, Shrimp, and Chinese Chives Dumplings

MAKES ABOUT 45 TO 50 DUMPLINGS

1 batch Dumpling Dough (page 67)

Balsamic-Soy Dipping Sauce (recipe follows), for serving

For the filling:

1 pound ground pork

¼ pound peeled and deveined gulf shrimp, roughly diced

½ cup chopped Chinese chives or leeks

2 teaspoons minced garlic

2 teaspoons minced fresh ginger

2 tablespoons soy sauce

1 tablespoon sesame oil

1 tablespoon Shaoxing wine or dry Marsala wine

Chinese chives are quite pungent, which gives these dumplings some kick. You can use the green or yellow variety. Chinese chives usually are sold in bunches. Incorporate any remaining chives in a stir-fry, fried rice, or stir-fried noodles.

- Make the dough according to the recipe. While the dough is resting, make the Balsamic-Soy Dipping Sauce and set aside.

- To make the filling, in the bowl of a food processor, put the pork, shrimp, chives, garlic, ginger, soy sauce, oil, and wine. Pulse for 5 seconds at a time until the filling is well combined. If needed, use a rubber spatula to scrape down the sides of the bowl. The ingredients should still be discernible and not pasty. Set the filling aside.

- Fill the wrappers with the prepared filling (see Making Dumplings, page 62).

- Boil, steam, or panfry the dumplings (see Cooking Dumplings, page 64), and serve with the dipping sauce.

Balsamic-Soy Dipping Sauce

MAKES ABOUT ½ CUP

⅓ cup soy sauce

¼ cup everyday balsamic vinegar

The sweetness from the balsamic helps to balance the saltiness of the soy sauce. You also can use Chinese black vinegar, combined with 1 teaspoon sugar.

■ In a small bowl, add the soy sauce and vinegar and stir to combine. You can store the dipping sauce in a sealed container in the refrigerator for up to 1 week.

牛肉酸菜餡

Beef with Chinese Mustard Greens Dumplings

MAKES ABOUT 45 TO 50 DUMPLINGS

1 batch Dumpling Dough (page 67)

Soy-Ginger Dipping Sauce (page 72), for serving

For the filling:

1 pound ground beef (80 percent lean)

2 cups finely chopped fresh Chinese mustard greens (leaves and stalks)

2 tablespoons soy sauce

1 tablespoon sesame oil

2 teaspoons minced garlic

2 teaspoons minced fresh ginger

The combination of beef and pickled Chinese mustard greens is a classic. But for this dumpling filling, I like the brightness of fresh Chinese mustard greens.

- Make the dough according to the recipe. While the dough is resting, make the Soy-Ginger Dipping Sauce and set aside.
- To make the filling, in a medium bowl, put the beef, greens, soy sauce, oil, garlic, and ginger, and stir to combine. Set the filling aside.
- Fill the wrappers with the prepared filling (see Making Dumplings, page 62).
- Boil, steam, or panfry the dumplings (see Cooking Dumplings, page 64), and serve with the dipping sauce.

NOTE: If you want to use pickled Chinese mustard greens, you can add 2 cups finely chopped to the beef instead of fresh. Make your own pickled greens (see page 157) or, if using store-bought, be sure to give them a quick rinse before cutting. If you like spice, add minced jalapeño to taste to the filling.

雞蝦九層塔餡

Basil, Chicken, and Shrimp Dumplings

MAKES ABOUT 45 TO 50 DUMPLINGS

1 batch Dumpling Dough (page 67)

Balsamic-Soy Dipping Sauce (page 75), for serving

For the filling:

1 pound ground chicken

¼ pound peeled and deveined gulf shrimp, roughly diced

1 cup loosely packed chopped fresh basil

2 tablespoons soy sauce

1 tablespoon sesame oil

1 tablespoon Shaoxing wine or dry Marsala wine

2 stalks green onions, chopped

2 teaspoons minced garlic

2 teaspoons minced fresh ginger

This combination is inspired by a dish called Three-Cup Chicken (page 152), named for its sauce made from one part each of soy sauce, rice wine, and sesame oil. The basil, which is not typical in Chinese cooking, is the surprise ingredient. I wanted to draw from those flavors to create a chicken filling that has some dimension. These dumplings taste great panfried as a pot sticker.

▪ Make the dough according to the recipe. While the dough is resting, make the Balsamic-Soy Dipping Sauce and set aside.

▪ To make the filling, in the bowl of a food processor, put the chicken, shrimp, basil, soy sauce, oil, wine, onions, garlic, and ginger. Pulse for 5 seconds at a time until the filling is well combined. If needed, use a rubber spatula to scrape down the sides of the bowl. The ingredients should still be discernible and not pasty. Set the filling aside.

▪ Fill the wrappers with the prepared filling (see Making Dumplings, page 62).

▪ Boil, steam, or panfry the dumplings (see Cooking Dumplings, page 64), and serve with the dipping sauce.

小吃

Little Eats

If you ever visit Taiwan or China, or a large city with a bustling Chinatown, you will understand the wonderland that comprises dozens upon dozens of little eats—or *xiao chi*. Similar to tapas or the small plates concept, little eats represent snacks or bowl foods that you would find at a street stall. They can be savory or sweet, a light bite or something more substantial. It's not formal food, and it's usually inexpensive. From the Western perspective, some of the little eats would classify as appetizers. But the Chinese wouldn't necessarily serve these foods as starters—not that it would be wrong. These foods are their own category.

Typically, little eats aren't made at home. In Asia, *xiao chi* stalls are ubiquitous, delicious, and usually specialize in one or two items. My mother's younger brother and his family have run a soy milk shop in Taiwan for decades. They press their own soy milk, which is served in a bowl warm or chilled, savory or sweet. They also make *shao bing you tiao*, the sesame flatbread and savory doughnut sandwich that people dip into their soy milk. The last time I was in Taiwan, I visited their shop, which has since changed locations, and watched them swiftly make the bread and doughnuts, which actually look more like puffy breadsticks, and ladle steaming bowls of soy milk for customers who would either grab one of the plastic stools and quickly eat their breakfast or hang the plastic baggie full of yumminess on their moped handles and zip off to work. It was so efficient yet so vital. When I was the featured cooking instructor on a cruise to China, one of the ports of call was outside of Beijing. My husband and mother were able to join me on the trip. We stayed the night at a Western-style hotel, but outside, around the corner in an alley, was a steamed-bun cart that sold these stunning bundles of juicy pork bao. I think we ordered half a dozen, and they were handed to us unceremoniously in a plastic bag. On that same trip, one of our ports was Dalian, in northeastern China. My mother hadn't been back to Mainland China since her family fled in 1949 when the Communists took over. Dalian was close to my mother's village, so it was poignant. But it wasn't until we came across a street vendor roasting sweet potatoes in a steel drum that my mother traveled back to her childhood. It was a steaming-hot roasted sweet potato, wrapped in paper, with no seasonings other than what the earth gave it. Mom had to suck in air to eat it without burning her tongue, and it was the best sweet potato she'd ever tasted.

One of these days, I'll have collected enough little eats recipes to fill a book. For now, I'll share some family favorites.

烤番薯

Just a Roasted Sweet Potato

MAKES 2 SERVINGS

2 medium sweet potatoes (about 1 pound)

My mother loves to eat roasted sweet potatoes as an occasional snack. She also enjoys eating them with Simple Congee (page 118) for a hearty breakfast. If you serve this with congee, you can pair it with Simple Stir-Fried Greens (page 137) for a savory counterpoint.

■ Preheat the oven to 425 degrees F.

■ Scrub the potatoes and pat dry with a paper towel. Pierce each potato in several places with a fork. Wrap each potato in foil and place them on a baking sheet. Bake for 45 to 55 minutes, or until soft and the sweet juices start to ooze. The cooking time may vary depending on the size of the potatoes. Let the potatoes cool, then unwrap them and serve.

醃拍小黃瓜

Smacked Cucumber

MAKES ABOUT 4 CUPS

5 to 6 Persian cucumbers or 1 small English cucumber

2 tablespoons soy sauce

1 tablespoon balsamic vinegar

1 teaspoon sugar

3 cloves garlic, crushed

¼ teaspoon red pepper flakes or 1 teaspoon finely chopped fresh chili pepper (optional)

This is perhaps more of a side dish or condiment than a little eat. But it's so refreshing and savory that you'd probably end up eating a large enough portion to qualify as a full-fledged *xiao chi*. I prefer using small Persian cucumbers. In season, I look for Japanese cucumbers at the farmers' market. The so-called cocktail cucumbers that you see packaged in small plastic totes work too. The name of the dish comes from the sound the cleaver makes when smacking cucumber pieces.

▪ Trim the ends of the cucumbers. Starting at one end of a cucumber, place the flat of your knife on top of the cucumber. Gently but firmly strike the blade with the heel of your palm to smash the cucumber into pieces. Repeat this for the rest of the cucumbers. If there are any large sections, you can cut through them.

▪ Put the smashed cucumbers in a medium bowl. Add the soy sauce, vinegar, sugar, garlic, and red pepper flakes, and mix well. Cover and let the cucumbers marinate on the counter for at least 30 minutes before serving. Store the cucumber in the refrigerator, covered, for up to 3 days.

滷蛋

Marbled Soy Sauce Eggs

MAKES 12 EGGS

12 large eggs

1 cup soy sauce

1 star anise

½ cinnamon stick

½ teaspoon whole Sichuan peppercorns

These eggs make a great snack or can be served as an accompaniment for a noodle soup or Red-Braised Pork Belly (page 187) and rice.

■ Place the eggs in a large pot. Add water until the eggs are covered by about 1 inch. Bring to a boil over high heat. Reduce the heat to low and let simmer for 8 minutes.

■ Remove the eggs, reserving the water. Run the eggs under cold water for 1 minute to make the shells easier to handle. Crack the shells all over gently with the back of a spoon, but don't break off the shells. You want to create a marbling effect around the entire egg.

■ Add the soy sauce, star anise, cinnamon, and peppercorns to the reserved cooking water. Add the cracked eggs back into the pot. Bring to a boil over high heat, then quickly reduce the heat to low, and let simmer for about 15 minutes.

■ Transfer the eggs and liquid to a large container with a lid, or use a large bowl and plastic wrap. Let the eggs steep in the refrigerator overnight, or up to two days (the longer they steep, the more pronounced the marbling). Peel the eggs to reveal the marbling, and serve. The eggs can be stored in the refrigerator for up to three days.

炒鍋煎蛋淋醬油

Wok-Fried Egg

with Soy Sauce

MAKES 1 SERVING

1 large egg

1 teaspoon vegetable oil

½ teaspoon soy sauce

Chopped fresh cilantro, chopped green onions, and chili sauce, for serving (optional)

1 slice toast, for serving

It may seem unnecessary to include a recipe for a fried egg, but it's sometimes the most familiar foods that deserve a little extra attention. My mother always made us fried eggs in a wok. Because the oil pools in a round-bottom wok, when the egg hits the oil, the white puffs up just a bit and starts to brown, and the edges crisp perfectly. A drizzle of soy sauce completes the picture. The other kids at school had never heard of adding soy sauce to a fried egg. Even then, I knew they were missing out. To eat the egg, I use chopsticks to pierce the yolk first to let the soy sauce mingle with the yolk. Then I separate the egg white in half, gather it up with the chopsticks, and sop up some of the yolk before eating. The Vietnamese serve fried egg and soy sauce with a piece of baguette. Since I don't live within walking distance of a French bakery, I keep it simple with a piece of everyday wheat toast. You can also serve this with Simple Congee (page 118).

▪ In a small bowl, carefully crack the egg, being careful not to break the yolk.

▪ Preheat a wok over medium heat for about 1 minute. Add the oil and heat for about 5 seconds, or until it starts to shimmer. Pour the egg into the oil. Let the bottom brown for about 30 seconds, or until you see the edges of the egg white start to turn golden. Gently flip the egg. Cook the egg yolk to desired doneness, 30 to 60 seconds.

▪ Transfer the egg to a plate. Drizzle with the soy sauce; top with the cilantro, green onion, and chili sauce; and serve with the toast to soak up the yolk.

豬肉鮮蝦燒賣

Pork and Shrimp Shao Mai

MAKES ABOUT 40 DUMPLINGS

- ¼ pound peeled and deveined fresh shrimp
- ¾ pound ground pork
- 2 stalks green onions, finely chopped
- 1 tablespoon soy sauce
- 1 teaspoon Shaoxing wine or dry Marsala wine
- ½ teaspoon sesame oil
- ½ teaspoon white pepper powder
- 1 package round dumpling wrappers (see note)
- Soy-Ginger Dipping Sauce (page 72), for serving
- Chili sauce, for serving

Shao mai, which you may recognize from dim sum restaurants as *siu mai* or *shu mai*, are basically meatballs wrapped in a noodle. Out of all the dumplings, this is probably the least challenging and most forgiving to make. Since the shrimp will be chopped up, the size and variety of shrimp is not as important as the freshness. Ask your fishmonger to help you choose the best option. For a splurge—and if you have access to them in season—you can use sweet-and-meaty spot prawns. You can try other filling combinations, such as chicken and scallops or pork and crab. You also can use the filling from the Basil, Chicken, and Shrimp Dumplings (page 77) for this recipe as an alternative.

▪ Cut the shrimp into a fine dice. In a large bowl, put the shrimp, pork, onions, soy sauce, wine, oil, and pepper, and stir well to combine. (Alternatively, put the shrimp in the bowl of a food processor. Pulse for 5 to 10 seconds, or until the shrimp is roughly chopped. Add the pork, green onions, soy sauce, wine, oil, and pepper, and pulse for a few seconds at a time until everything is combined but not pasty, then scrape the filling mixture into a large bowl.)

▪ Line a baking sheet with parchment paper. Set aside.

▪ Place about 1 heaping teaspoon of filling in the center of a dumpling wrapper. Gather the wrapper around the filling, making sure the sides adhere to the filling but not sealing the top. It will look like a little cup. Place the dumpling on the prepared baking sheet. Repeat with the remaining wrappers and filling.

▪ Set up your steamer (see page 47). Cooking in batches, place the dumplings in a single layer in the steamer, and steam for 8 to 9 minutes, until the wrappers are translucent. Serve immediately with the dipping sauce and your choice of chili sauce. (If you aren't cooking all the dumplings right away, you can store them in the freezer in a single layer on a baking sheet for about 1 hour to set. Then transfer them to a freezer bag, and store in the freezer for up to two weeks. To serve, do not defrost the dumplings but steam them for an extra minute or so.)

NOTE: The round dumpling wrappers may be labeled "gyoza" or "pot sticker" or "siu mai" wrappers. Sometimes, they come in different thicknesses. Stick with thin or regular wrappers. If your market doesn't carry the round dumpling wrappers, you can use the square wonton wrappers instead.

撇拉絲拌包心菜絲

Green Cabbage and Kohlrabi Slaw

MAKES ABOUT 4 TO 6 SERVINGS

1 medium kohlrabi (about ¾ pound), trimmed and cut into 2-inch-long, thin strips

1 medium carrot, trimmed and cut into 2-inch-long strips

2 cups thinly sliced green cabbage

1 teaspoon kosher salt

For the dressing:

2 tablespoons plus 1½ teaspoons rice vinegar

2 tablespoons soy sauce

1 teaspoon sugar

1 teaspoon Chili Oil (page 99) or ½ teaspoon red pepper flakes

My mother is retired and lives with me and my family. During the day, when the kids are at school and my husband and I are at work, Mom hangs out at home, surfs the web, writes life essays for her blog (in Mandarin), and occasionally improvises dishes, such as this salad for her lunch. Curious about kohlrabi, she had bought one but then let it languish a bit in the produce bin. When she finally got around to using it, she peeled the kohlrabi, cut it into thin strips, and paired it with a quarter of a green cabbage that was leftover from one of my cooking projects. Kohlrabi has a mild flavor but offers great crunch. The acid in the dressing comes from unseasoned rice vinegar. Mom added a dash of chili oil, just because the jar happened to be sitting on the counter. Serve the slaw as a salad before the main course or as an accompaniment to a heavier meal.

■ In a large mixing bowl, combine the kohlrabi, carrot, and cabbage. Add the salt and, using clean hands, work the salt into the vegetables. Cover the bowl with plastic wrap and let it sit in the refrigerator for at least 1 hour and up to overnight. (This process will help the vegetables release some of their liquid.) Do not drain the liquid.

■ To make the dressing, in a small bowl, combine the vinegar, soy sauce, sugar, and oil, and stir to dissolve the sugar. Add the dressing to the slaw and mix well. Taste for seasoning, adding more salt if needed. Serve right away. The slaw also can be covered and stored in the refrigerator for up to a week.

蔥油餅

Green Onion Pancakes

MAKES 4 (6-INCH) PANCAKES

- 1 batch Dumpling Dough (page 67)
- 5 tablespoons vegetable oil, plus more for coating the dough
- About 2 teaspoons kosher salt, divided
- 4 stalks green onions, finely chopped
- Soy-Ginger Dipping Sauce (page 72), for serving

When I was a child, I loved green onion pancakes—but not the actual green onions. The flavor they imparted was wonderful, but the onions themselves were too pungent for my taste. So I used to pick out as many of the green onion pieces as I could before I'd eat the pancake. I don't have an issue with green onions anymore. Coincidentally, my daughter will not go near green onions except in green onion pancakes.

If making ahead of time, place the raw formed pancakes on a parchment-lined baking sheet. Freeze them for about an hour and then transfer the pancakes to a freezer bag; store them in the freezer for up to two weeks. Do not defrost the pancakes before cooking. If you have a griddle, you can make larger pancakes. If you roll them out to the size of a large tortilla and slightly undercook them so that they remain pliable, you can use them as a wrap for the Sliced Red-Braised Beef Shank (page 189).

▪ Divide the dough into quarters. Roll a section out to about 8½ inches in diameter. Brush a coating of oil on the dough. Sprinkle about ½ teaspoon salt across the oiled dough. Sprinkle on 2 to 3 tablespoons of onions. Starting from the bottom edge of the round of dough, roll the dough tightly into a tube, then take one end and create a tightly wound coil. Tuck the end under the coil. Now, roll the coil flat until it's about 6½ inches in diameter and ⅛ inch thick. Repeat with the remaining sections of dough.

▪ Preheat an 8-inch skillet over medium-low heat for about 1 minute. Add 2 tablespoons oil and heat for about 5 seconds, or until it starts to shimmer. Add a pancake and fry for 1½ to 2 minutes, or until golden. Flip and repeat. Remove the pancake and set aside on a plate. Add 1 tablespoon of oil to the pan before cooking each of the remaining pancakes. Cut the pancakes into wedges and serve with the dipping sauce.

芹菜牛肉餡餅

Beef and Celery Hearts Meat Pies

(Xian Bing)

MAKES 8 MEAT PIES

2 cups all-purpose flour

½ cup plus 1 tablespoon hot tap water (about 110 to 115 degrees F), divided

For the filling:

½ pound ground beef

½ cup finely chopped celery hearts (innermost yellow stalks)

2 stalks green onions, finely chopped

1 tablespoon plus 1½ teaspoons soy sauce

¼ teaspoon white pepper powder

2 tablespoons plus 1 teaspoon vegetable oil, divided

1 teaspoon kosher salt

Soy sauce, for serving

Chili Oil (page 99) or your favorite chili sauce, for serving

These meat pies, called *xian bing*, have a double crust, and they're not intimidating to shape because there's no pleating involved. I like the combination of beef and celery hearts. You have to use the inner, lightest-yellow stalks, which are the most tender. You can even eat the leaves. Be careful when you bite into one, though, because the juices may shoot out.

■ Put the flour in a medium bowl. Gradually add ½ cup of the water while mixing with a fork or spatula. Once the flour starts to clump, start gathering the pieces with your hand to make a ball. If the dough feels too dry, work in the remaining 1 tablespoon water. The dough should feel tacky but it shouldn't stick to your fingers. Knead the dough for 1 minute. Cover the bowl loosely with plastic wrap, and set aside to rest while you make the filling.

■ To make the filling, in an medium bowl, put the beef, celery, onions, soy sauce, and pepper, and mix well. Set aside.

■ Knead the dough for 1 to 2 minutes more, or until smooth. Divide the dough in half. Roll out one piece of dough into a circle about ¼ inch thick. The diameter is not important. Brush ½ teaspoon of the oil on the surface. Sprinkle ½ teaspoon of the salt across the dough. Starting from the edge closest to you, roll the dough into a tube. This will help to create some layers. Cut the tube into four equal pieces. Set aside. Repeat with the other half of the dough.

■ Take a dough piece and gently press it into a ball. Roll it out to about 4 inches in diameter, like a mini pizza. Add 1 heaping tablespoon of filling in the center. Seal the dough around the filling, pinching the edges together, then gently press the ball into a puck-like shape roughly 2½ inches in diameter and about 1 to 1¼ inch thick. Repeat with the remaining pieces of dough.

■ Preheat an 8- to 10-inch cast-iron skillet or a nonstick pan over medium-low heat for about 1 minute. Add 1 tablespoon of the oil per four bings. If you can fit all eight in a single pan, great; if not, cook them in batches. Let the oil heat for about 30 seconds, or until shimmering. Add the bings but do not let the sides touch. They won't expand, but you don't want them to stick together. Cook, covered, for 3 to 4 minutes per side, or until both sides are crusty and the color is a rich golden brown. If they start to brown too quickly, adjust the heat. Serve with soy sauce and chili oil.

芝麻燒餅

Sesame Flatbread

(Shao Bing)

MAKES 8 FLATBREADS

For the roux:

¼ cup vegetable oil

¼ cup all-purpose flour

3 cups all-purpose flour, plus more for dusting

⅔ cup boiling water

⅓ cup cold tap water

1 to 2 tablespoons warm tap water, if needed

1 teaspoon kosher salt

¼ cup sesame seeds

¼ cup water

I learned the basic recipe for this breakfast flatbread from my uncle, whose family runs a tiny *shao bing* shop in Taichung, Taiwan. People line up every morning to get a *shao bing you tiao* (*you tiao* are "savory doughnuts") sandwich with a bowl of sweet or savory soy milk. It's a ubiquitous breakfast. I like to fill the bread with an egg scramble seasoned with whatever Chinese greens I have in my fridge, or eat it with Tomato Egg (page 141). My kids eat *shao bing* toasted and topped with butter. My husband calls *shao bing* Chinese Pop-Tarts. More ways to eat *shao bing*: as a sandwich with braised beef (see page 191), toasted and filled with red bean paste, toasted and buttered, or dipped in Hot-and-Sour Soup (page 170).

■ To make the roux, in a small pan over medium heat, heat the oil for 1 minute, or until the surface starts to shimmer slightly. Add the flour and, using a heatproof spatula or a small whisk, stir quickly to combine. Reduce the heat to low. Stir the mixture constantly for about 3 minutes, or until the color of the roux resembles peanut butter. Remove the pan from the heat. Continue to stir for about 1 minute, letting the residual heat from the pan brown the roux even more. Scrape the roux into a heatproof bowl and set aside.

■ Put the flour in a large bowl. Add the boiling water and, using a spatula or a wooden spoon, stir quickly to distribute. Add the cold water and stir to combine. As the dough forms, you can use your hands to start bringing the dough together. If it feels too dry, you can add the warm tap water. Once you've worked all the flour into the mound of dough, take the dough out of the bowl and knead it on a work surface for about 2 minutes, or until smooth. The dough should feel damp but not sticky.

■ Lightly dust your work surface with flour. Roll out the dough into a rectangle about 18 inches long by 12 inches wide and ¼ inch thick; be sure the longer edge is parallel to the edge of your work surface. Stir the roux a few times. Using a spatula or large spoon, spread about 4 tablespoons of the roux on the dough, leaving a ½-inch border around the edge. Sprinkle the salt over the roux. (It may seem like it's too much salt, but it isn't.)

■ Starting from the longer edge of the rectangle, roll the dough into a cylinder, then seal the ends by pinching the edges together to create a seam. Cut the cylinder of dough into eight equal segments.

→

- Preheat the oven to 450 degrees F. Line a baking sheet with parchment paper. Set aside.

- Turn each segment of the dough so that the seam is on the bottom and the cut edge (where you see the coil of dough) is facing you. Roll out the dough into a rectangle about 5 inches long by 3½ inches wide and ¼ inch thick. Flip the rectangle so that the seam side is now facing up. Trifold the rectangle as if you were folding a letter. With the folded edge perpendicular to you, roll out the dough again into a rectangle about 5 inches long by 3½ inches wide. Repeat the trifold and set aside, with the flap facing down. Repeat with the remaining pieces of dough.

- Put the sesame seeds on a small plate. Brush a little water on the surface of each piece of dough. Dip the moistened sides into the sesame seeds. With the seed side up, roll each dough into a rectangle about 5 inches long by 3 inches wide and ¼ inch thick. Place the bread on the prepared baking sheet. Repeat with the remaining dough. Bake for 15 minutes, then flip the breads and bake for 4 minutes more, or until the breads puff up and have a lightly browned color on the surface.

- Remove the breads from the oven and let them cool slightly before serving.

餛飩

Wontons

MAKES ABOUT 40 TO 45 WONTONS

- 1 pound ground chicken
- 2 stalks green onions, finely chopped
- 1 tablespoon soy sauce
- ½ teaspoon sesame oil
- ⅛ teaspoon white pepper powder
- 1 package wonton wrappers
- Chili Sauce for Wontons (recipe follows)

My first job after my parents opened a Chinese restaurant was to make wontons. I was eight when I started folding wontons for the restaurant, and it was my job until I left home at twenty-four with a journalism degree for a job in the big city two states away. When I got bored with the repetition, I would time myself to see how long it would take me to fill a tray. My record was something like ninety-six wontons in about twelve minutes. It took a long time after I left home before I could enjoy eating wontons again. You can boil the wontons and serve right away with Chili Sauce for Wontons (recipe follows), use them for Wonton Soup (page 178), or deep-fry them. You also can freeze the wontons and cook only the amount you need.

■ In a medium bowl, put the chicken, onions, soy sauce, oil, and pepper, and mix well.

■ Put ¼ cup water in a small bowl. Line a baking sheet with parchment paper. Set aside.

■ Place just under 1 teaspoon of the filling at the center of a wonton square. You will have to adjust the amount of filling as needed. Wonton skins can vary in dimension, so use your best judgment.

■ Dip your finger in the water and moisten all four edges as if you are sealing an envelope flap. Fold the wrapper in half over the filling, line up the edges, and press down to flatten and seal. You will now have a rectangle packet.

■ Pick up the filled rectangle and hold it so that the edge that contains the filling is at the bottom. Moisten the lower left corner of the rectangle. Using both hands, wrap the lower edges of the wonton into a small circle until they meet, and adhere the bottom right corner of the rectangle to the moistened left corner. Repeat with the remaining filling and wonton skins.

■ Place the wontons on the prepared baking sheet. (If you plan on freezing the wontons for later use, place the baking sheet in the freezer for about 1 hour before transferring the wontons to a ziplock bag. You can cook them frozen. Do not defrost or you will get a soggy mess.)

→

■ To cook the wontons, in an 8-quart pot, bring 3 quarts of water to a boil. Add 8 wontons per person and boil for 4 to 5 minutes, or until the wontons become opaque and the filling is cooked through. Drain the wontons and transfer them to bowls to serve. Drizzle 2 to 3 tablespoons of the Chili Sauce for Wontons, or more to taste, over each bowl, and serve.

Chili Sauce for Wontons

MAKES ABOUT ½ CUP

- 2 tablespoons chili bean sauce
- 1 stalk green onion, very finely minced
- 2 teaspoons Chili Oil (recipe follows)
- 1 teaspoon finely minced garlic
- 1 teaspoon sugar
- ½ teaspoon sesame oil
- ½ teaspoon freshly ground Sichuan peppercorn
- ½ cup soy sauce
- 1 tablespoon balsamic vinegar

There are many variations of this sauce, so you can adjust the flavors to your liking. I suggest experimenting with different brands of chili or chili bean sauces. For example, I like to use the Lee Kum brand chili black bean sauce, which has a great kick and a very savory flavor.

■ In a small bowl, combine the bean sauce, onion, Chili Oil, garlic, sugar, sesame oil, and peppercorn. Stir well. Add the soy sauce and balsamic vinegar. Stir to combine. This will keep in the refrigerator for up to a week.

Chili Oil

MAKES ABOUT ½ CUP

- ½ cup vegetable oil
- 1 medium shallot, finely minced
- 2 teaspoons freshly cracked Sichuan peppercorns
- 1 to 2 teaspoons red pepper flakes
- 1 to 2 teaspoons Chinese or Korean chili powder

Chili oil is not difficult to make and it tastes fresher than the bottled versions you find in Asian markets. Store the chili oil in an airtight glass jar in the pantry and use within two weeks. The spice level will vary according to the type of chili powder you buy, so be sure to read the chili powder label for the heat level. The oil becomes spicier as the chilies steep.

■ In a small pan over low heat, combine the oil, shallot, peppercorns, and pepper flakes and chili powder to taste, and cook for 5 minutes, or until the oil starts to look red from the chili. Remove the pan from the heat, then pour the oil into a small heatproof bowl and let cool to room temperature before storing in an airtight jar.

春捲

Spring Rolls

MAKES ABOUT 1 DOZEN

- 1 small bundle bean thread noodles, soaked in warm water to reconstitute
- 2 tablespoons vegetable oil, plus more for frying
- 2½ cups thinly sliced Chinese cabbage
- 1 medium carrot, cut into thin, 2-inch strips (about ¾ cup)
- 6 medium fresh or dried shiitake mushrooms (if using dried, soak in warm water to reconstitute), thinly sliced
- 2 stalks green onions, finely chopped
- ¼ cup water
- 3 tablespoons soy sauce
- Kosher salt
- ½ teaspoon sesame oil
- ½ cup chopped fresh cilantro (optional)
- 1 package spring roll wrappers
- 1 egg, beaten
- Sweet-and-Sour Sauce (page 222), for serving
- Soy sauce, for serving
- Chili sauce, for serving

For twenty-three years in the restaurant business, we served Americanized egg rolls filled with shredded green cabbage, onions, carrots, and celery, because our customers wanted cheap food and, in this case, a fried vehicle for sweet-and-sour sauce. (You can find Restaurant-Style Egg Rolls on page 221.) For our family, my mom made these spring rolls, which feature napa cabbage, shiitake mushrooms, and bean thread noodles. They have so much more flavor and, back then, I always wondered why we never shared our version.

■ Drain the bean thread. Cut the bean thread bundle into three to four segments so the noodles aren't whole but also aren't too short.

■ In a wok or large skillet, heat the vegetable oil over medium-high heat. Add the cabbage, carrots, mushrooms, and onions, and stir-fry the vegetables for about 1 minute, or until the cabbage has cooked through. Add the bean thread, water, and soy sauce, stir to combine, and cook for 2 to 3 minutes, or until the bean thread have absorbed the sauce. Add salt to taste. Drizzle with the sesame oil and add the cilantro. Give everything a good toss to combine. Transfer the filling to a large bowl and set aside to cool for a few minutes.

■ Position a sheet of spring roll wrapper with a corner toward you so that it's like a diamond. Place about ¼ cup filling about 2 inches above the bottom corner of the wrapper. Fold the bottom corner up over the filling and roll about halfway up. Fold the right side "flap" over the filling, then the left side. Brush the top flap with egg and then finish rolling to seal. Repeat with the remaining wrappers and filling.

■ In a deep pan, add about 1½ inches of vegetable oil, and heat over high heat to 375 degrees F on an instant-read thermometer. In two batches, fry the rolls for 2 minutes per side, or until the skin is evenly brown. If the skin browns too quickly, then the oil is too hot. Adjust the stove as needed.

■ Serve immediately with a selection of condiments, including sweet-and-sour sauce, soy sauce, and your favorite bottled chili sauce.

Hsiao-Ching
&

Hsiao-Ching
&

Hsiao-Ching
&

Hsiao-Ching
&

紅燒肉餡鍋貼

Red-Braised Pork Belly Pot Stickers

MAKES ABOUT 40 POT STICKERS

1 batch Dumpling Dough (page 67)

For the filling:

1 batch Red-Braised Pork Belly (page 187), chilled overnight (see note, page 104)

All-purpose flour, for dusting

1 cup chopped Pickled Chinese Mustard Greens (page 157) or store-bought, divided

1 cup finely chopped fresh cilantro, divided

1 cup peanut powder, divided

3 tablespoons vegetable oil

Ginger-Scallion Oil (recipe follows), for serving

Hot sauce, such as sriracha or *gochujang*, for serving

This recipe is a mash-up of three dishes I love: pork belly pinch buns (*gua bao*), pot stickers, and soup dumplings. I've taken the best parts of each and put them into one blast of flavor. There's the braised pork belly and condiments from the *gua bao*, the crispy skin of pot stickers, and the juiciness of soup dumplings. This dish requires some advance work, so plan accordingly. If you can't find peanut powder in your Asian market, grind about one cup of roasted unsalted peanuts into a powder (don't overgrind or you will get peanut butter) and then combine with one tablespoon of brown sugar. If you have an allergy, feel free to omit the peanut powder.

■ Make the dough according the recipe. While the dough is resting, prepare the filling.

■ Cut the chilled pork belly into slices that are roughly ¼ inch thick and ¾ inch wide. You may have to adjust the dimensions according to how large you end up rolling your wrappers. The braising liquid will have gelled overnight. You will need that gelatin for the filling.

■ Once the dough has rested, divide it in half. Roll each half into a rope that's about ¾ inch in diameter and about 18 inches in length. Using a knife or a bench scraper, cut each rope into pieces that are about 1 inch long. Each piece should weigh about 11 grams. Because the filling is so bulky, you are making the wrappers slightly larger than for regular pot stickers.

■ Roll each piece of dough into a small ball and then flatten it between your palms to create a disc that resembles a wafer cookie. Position your rolling pin between you and the base of the wafer of dough. Dust lightly with flour as needed. Roll the pin forward across the wafer of dough and back. You do not need to lift the rolling pin. Turn the dough 90 degrees and repeat the forward-and-back rolling. Turn the dough 90 degrees again and repeat the rolling. You will begin to see a circle forming. Repeat this process until the wrapper is a circle that's about 4½ inches in diameter.

■ Place 1 piece of pork belly, making sure there's some of the gelled braising liquid in the mix, on the wrapper. Top with pinches of the greens, cilantro, and a hearty sprinkle of the peanut powder (the total amount of

→

toppings should be about 1 teaspoon). Carefully pinch the edges of the wrapper together so that you create a half-moon shape. Repeat with the rest of the dough.

■ Preheat an 8- to 10-inch nonstick skillet over medium-high heat for about 1 minute. Add the vegetable oil, and swirl around the pan to coat. It's okay if there's a little bit of pooling. Place the dumplings in a single layer in the skillet. (You will need to cook the dumplings in batches.) Add ¾ cup water, cover, and cook for 7 to 9 minutes, or until the water has evaporated and the bottoms of the dumplings have browned and created that pot sticker crust. Transfer the pot stickers to a platter. If the pot stickers seem greasy, you may dab them on a paper towel before arranging on the platter. Repeat with the remaining dumplings.

■ Serve with the Ginger-Scallion Oil and hot sauce to taste. Be careful when taking the first bite, because the gelled braising liquid will have melted.

NOTE: After you have braised the pork belly, transfer the pieces of belly to a storage container. Strain and defat the braising liquid. Add the strained liquid back to the pork belly, and chill in the refrigerator overnight. The broth will become the gelatin that goes in the dumplings.

Ginger-Scallion Oil

MAKES ABOUT 1 CUP

- 2½ cups green onions, finely chopped (about 1 to 2 bunches)
- ½ cup freshly grated ginger
- ¼ cup vegetable oil
- 1 teaspoon kosher salt
- ¾ teaspoon rice vinegar

Use a neutral oil, such as canola, to make this recipe. The longer it sits, the more intense the flavor becomes.

■ In a medium bowl, combine the onions, ginger, oil, salt, and vinegar. Let sit on the counter for at least 30 minutes so that all the flavors can meld together. You can store the oil in the refrigerator for several days.

THE PERFECT BITE

Gua bao is a Taiwanese snack that's sometimes, oddly, translated to "pork hamburger." That is an injustice to this perfection of unctuous red-braised pork belly in a bready, taco shell–like bun. Combine that with Pickled Chinese Mustard Greens (page 157), cilantro, hot sauce, and peanut powder, and you have a sandwich you won't soon forget. To make *gua bao*, you will need 1 package of steamed folded buns, which are available in the freezer aisle of an Asian market. They usually come in a pack of about a dozen. Steam them per the package's directions. Follow the directions in the Red-Braised Pork Belly Pot Stickers recipe (page 103) but omit the dumpling dough and dumpling-making instructions. In each steamed bun, add a slice of the pork belly, 1 teaspoon of chopped Pickled Chinese Mustard Greens, ½ teaspoon peanut powder, cilantro, and hot sauce of your choice. Eat.

小籠湯包

Soup Dumplings

(Xiao Long Bao)

MAKES ABOUT 40

For the gelatin:

2 pounds unsmoked, skin-on pork hock (see note, page 109)

½ pound pork skin (recommended, but optional)

1 pound chicken carcasses, if available, or parts such as drumsticks and wings

2 stalks green onions, cut into 3-inch segments

3 slices fresh ginger

¼ cup soy sauce

¼ cup Shaoxing wine or dry Marsala wine

Kosher salt

3 quarts water, plus more as needed

1 (¼-ounce) envelope Knox gelatin (optional)

For the dough:

2 cups all-purpose flour, plus more for dusting

½ cup bread flour

¾ cup plus 1 tablespoon hot water (150 to 160 degrees F)

When it comes to soup dumplings, you are just as likely to see a street vendor in Shanghai selling them in plastic bags to office workers as you are to see lines of people outside of famous full-service restaurants such as the many Din Tai Fung locations around the world. The Chinese don't typically make soup dumplings at home, because it's something that we enjoy at a restaurant or at a street stall. That said, it is possible to make them at home if you are patient and willing.

There are a few schools of thought when it comes to making the gelatin and the dough. For example, some people add powdered gelatin or agar-agar to chicken stock to make the filling. I prefer to simmer pork skin (which I buy directly from a local farmer), skin-on pork hocks, and chicken bones. The skin yields collagen that naturally gels when chilled. When it comes to the dough, some cooks use just all-purpose flour. Others use a combination of all-purpose and bread flours. Another version mixes in a pinch of a yeasted starter dough with cake and all-purpose flours. I've tried many incarnations of each part of this recipe, and the following method works best for me.

It's easier to serve soup dumplings directly from the steamer baskets. You will need at least two ten-inch baskets, so that one can steam while you continue to fill the second with dumplings. Then the first basket can be served while the second is steaming. The process for making soup dumplings will take two days, so plan ahead.

▪ To make the gelatin, put the pork hock, pork skin, chicken carcasses, onions, ginger, soy sauce, wine, and salt to taste in a stock pot. Add the water, adding more as needed to make sure it covers all of the ingredients. Bring to a boil over high heat and then reduce the heat to low. Simmer for 2 to 3 hours, or until the broth is reduced by at least half and the consistency has thickened from the collagen; it will resemble a slurry. You will have to check it from time to time and gently shift the hocks and chicken to prevent any sticking. After 2 hours, add additional salt to taste. Let cool slightly and strain the broth into a 2-quart glass baking dish (or other similar heatproof container). Let the broth cool to room temperature, cover, and then chill in the refrigerator overnight. The gelatin should be quite firm. If it's not, it will make your filling too damp and very challenging to use.

→

For the filling:

1 pound ground pork

2 tablespoons soy sauce

2 stalks green onions, finely chopped

1 teaspoon grated or finely minced fresh ginger

1 teaspoon white pepper powder

1 teaspoon sesame oil

Black Vinegar with Chili-Garlic Sauce (recipe follows), or black vinegar and finely julienned fresh ginger, for serving

■ If, the next day, the gelatin still jiggles when you shake the pan, here's how to correct it: In a pot over medium heat, melt the gelatin. Add the Knox gelatin into the broth gelatin, and stir to dissolve. Transfer to the baking dish and chill until firm.

■ Cut the gelatin into ¼-inch dice and place in a medium bowl. Cover with plastic wrap and set aside in the refrigerator.

■ To make the dough, put the flours in a large bowl, and stir to combine. Gradually add half the water while stirring with a spatula or a pair of chopsticks. As the dough comes together, add more water. You may or may not need all of the water. Press the dough together; if you can form a ball, you can stop adding water. Form a ball and knead the dough for about 4 minutes, or until smooth. Cover the bowl with a damp towel and let the dough rest for 30 minutes at room temperature.

■ To make the filling, in the bowl of a food processor, put the pork, soy sauce, onions, ginger, and pepper. Pulse about five to six times to mix the meat and to create a fluffy texture. Add the oil and the gelatin. Pulse two to three times just until the gelatin becomes incorporated. Do not overprocess or the filling will become too pasty. Transfer the filling to a medium bowl, cover with plastic wrap, and set aside in the refrigerator until ready to use.

■ Line a baking sheet with parchment paper and set aside. Line the steamer baskets with perforated parchment paper and set up the steamer (see page 47).

■ On a lightly floured work surface, knead the dough again for 2 minutes, or until smooth. Divide the dough into two portions. Cover one half with a damp towel. Roll the other half into a rope about 1 inch in diameter. Cut rope into pieces about 1 inch long or about 10 grams each. With a Chinese rolling pin (dowel), roll out each piece of dough into a 3½-inch round. Place about 1 tablespoon of filling in the center of the wrapper. Gather the edges and twist into a "topknot" above the center of the dumpling (see photo on page 106). Place each dumpling in the steamer basket, leaving about 1 inch of space between dumplings. Repeat with the remaining dough and filling. If you don't have enough steamer baskets, place the sealed dumplings on the lined baking sheet.

■ Steam the dumplings (see page 65) over high heat for 6 to 8 minutes, depending on the size of the dumplings. When done steaming, the dough will transform from opaque to slightly translucent.

■ Serve immediately, straight from the basket, with the chili-garlic sauce.

NOTE: It is important to choose hocks that have the skin (or rind) fully intact. The collagen from the skin is what helps to thicken the broth and causes it to gel hard.

On another note, if you have access to a farmer at your local farmers' market who sells high-quality pork, ask if he or she can get you some pork skin. For example, I asked one of the owners of Skagit River Ranch, which is located north of Seattle, if she would sell me pork skin. It took her a few weeks to turn it around, but she was able to get me some. The quality difference is striking. I have found that the pork skin that I am able to buy from the Asian market likely comes from feedlot pigs. The skin tends to have a gamey, off flavor that's unpleasant in the broth. The product I get from Skagit River Ranch's pasture-raised pigs has a clean aroma, so the broth is untainted.

Black Vinegar with Chili-Garlic Sauce

MAKES ABOUT ½ CUP

½ cup Chinese black vinegar or balsamic vinegar

1 tablespoon chili bean sauce

2 large cloves garlic, finely minced or crushed

1 teaspoon soy sauce

This is a flexible recipe that can be made as vinegary or spicy as you please. If you want to add a hint of sweetness, use balsamic vinegar instead of black vinegar.

- In a small bowl, combine the vinegar, bean sauce, garlic, and soy sauce. You can store this sauce in the refrigerator for up to 1 week.

HOW TO EAT A SOUP DUMPLING

You have to eat a soup dumpling while it's still steaming hot. You need a pair of chopsticks, a sauce dish with black vinegar and ginger, and a Chinese soupspoon or other deep spoon. Gently use your chopsticks to lift the soup dumpling by the topknot. Be careful not to puncture the skin to avoid spilling out the melted gelatin, which is now the eponymous soup. Quickly dip the dumpling in the vinegar-ginger sauce and then place it in your spoon. Take a small bite from the top of the dumpling and suck out the soup, being cautious of the potentially scalding temperature. Then eat the rest of the dumpling. Some people take a bite first and then spoon in some dipping sauce. It's up to you. Personally, I prefer to put the entire soup dumpling in my mouth so that when I bite into it, the soup and dumpling create the perfect bite. That, however, takes skill to keep from burning your tongue.

米飯和麵條

Rice and Noodles

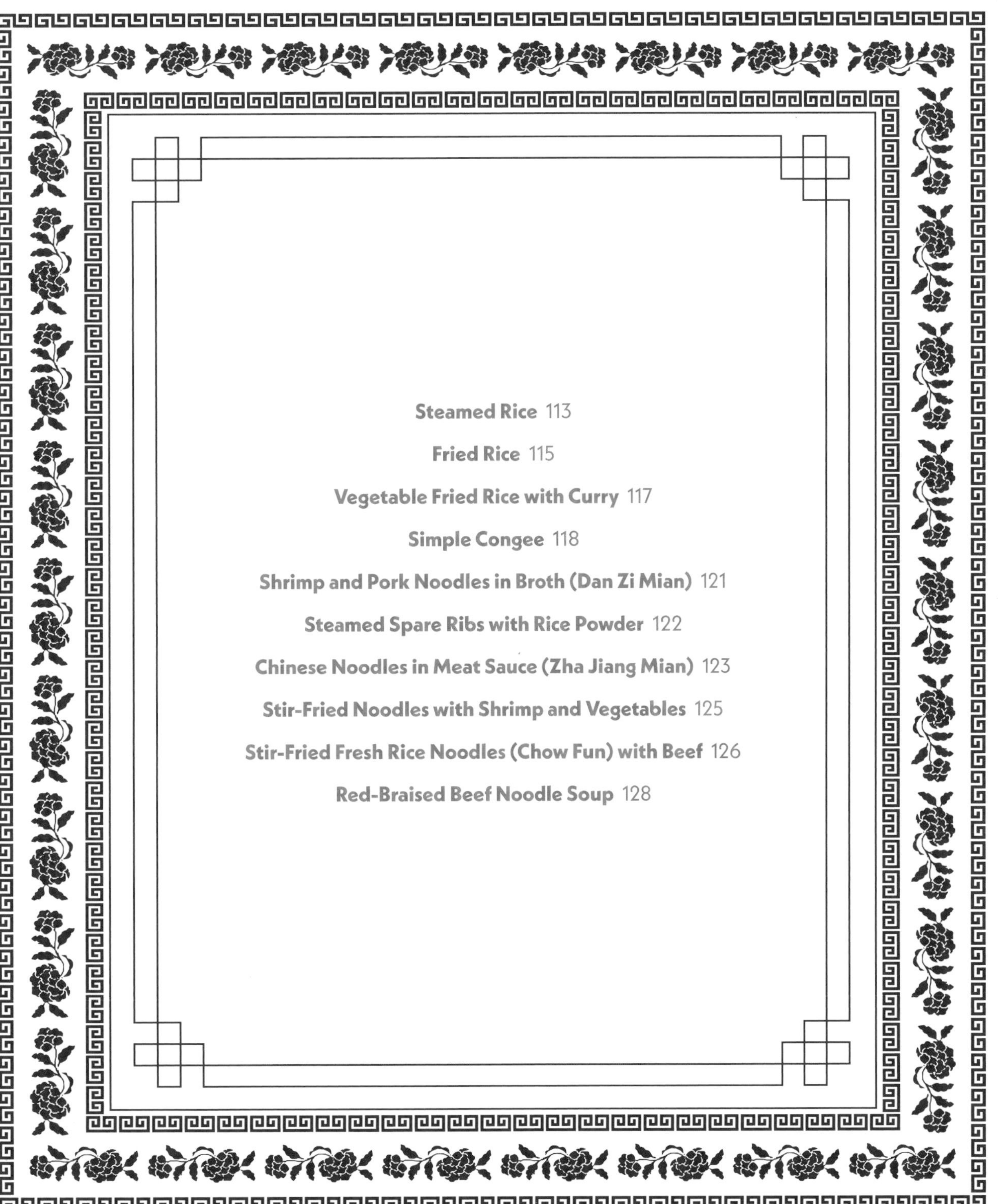

Rice is so central to the Chinese culture that we greet one another by asking, *"Ni chi fan le ma?"* Literally translated, it means "have you eaten rice yet?" I love the warmth and hospitality of the question, and the implication that when people get together, they ought to do so over a shared meal. This custom is universal, transcending socioeconomic status, geography, and regional dialects. Rice is an anchor. When my father took us on a family trip to Europe back in the early 1990s, he somehow found a Chinese restaurant in each town, from Paris to Lausanne to Florence. He loved to travel and see new lands, but when it came to dinner, he needed his bowl of rice. And how wonderful that the diaspora of Chinese restaurants could oblige.

This reverence for rice hits a different note in the West, where rice is a blank canvas for copious amounts of sauce. Even in my own home, there is a sauce divide. Where my mother and I consider stir-fry an accompaniment that enhances the fragrance of rice, my husband and children aim first for as much sauce as possible. If I make a dish that doesn't generate enough sauce, the disappointment is swift. The star and the canvas, rice binds us all around the table.

Noodles hold a similar position of esteem, especially in the northern half of China, where wheat grows and wheat products—noodles, buns, dumplings—reign. Rice, however, is cultivated in southern China, where the climate is more conducive. The journal *Science* published a study describing how the personalities of northerners and southerners are influenced by the wheat-rice divide. Apparently, the heartier northern noodle eaters are more individualistic, whereas the southern rice eaters are more interdependent. Luckily, my ancestors came from all along the noodle-rice continuum and passed down to me a love for both.

白飯

Steamed Rice

MAKES 4 CUPS

2 cups medium- or long-grain white rice (see note)

2½ cups water

To say that I rely on a rice cooker and never make rice on the stovetop probably isn't helpful. But that's the reality. Nowadays, you can spend as much on a rice cooker as a mobile device, and it will offer numerous settings for different rice varieties and preparations. For those who don't own a rice cooker, here is a basic stovetop method for steamed rice. I grew up eating long-grain Jasmine rice, but I have adopted a taste for short- or medium-grain Japanese rice because I enjoy the glutinous quality. The type of grain will determine the exact cooking time. For reference, look on the package of the rice you buy for specific cooking instructions. I don't salt the water, as is common practice in the West, because the accompanying stir-fry or other dishes are considered "condiments."

■ Put the rice in a large fine-mesh sieve or colander with small holes. Rinse the rice for about 1 minute under running water.

■ Put the rice in a 2-quart pot with a heavy bottom. Add the water, and cover the pot with a lid. (If you plan ahead, you can let the rice soak for 30 minutes to help the cooking process; heat penetrates soaked rice more easily.) Bring to a boil over high heat, which should take about 3 minutes. (Don't walk away from the stove, because the pot could easily boil over.) Reduce the heat to low. Cock the lid slightly to let the steam escape as you cook. Continue to cook for 25 to 30 minutes more, or until all the water has been absorbed and the rice is no longer soggy. Remove the pot from the heat and let the rice rest in the pot, covered, for at least 10 to 15 minutes to let the rice finish steaming. Transfer to a serving bowl and serve.

NOTE: For brown rice, follow the instructions above, but cook on low for a total of 30 to 35 minutes. Let the rice rest, covered, for 15 to 20 minutes before serving.

MAKING CONGEE

There will be a layer of rice that's stuck to the bottom of the pot. You can make a simple congee by adding 3 cups of water to the pot. Bring to a boil over high heat. As the water is heating, use a wooden spoon to gently scrape the rice off the pot. When the water comes to a boil, reduce the heat to low. Using a wooden spoon, gently scrape the rice. Let simmer for about 20 minutes, or until thick, stirring on occasion to prevent sticking. See Simple Congee (page 118) for condiment suggestions.

炒飯

Fried Rice

MAKES 4 SERVINGS

- 5 cups cold cooked rice
- 2 tablespoons vegetable oil, divided
- 2 eggs, beaten
- 2 stalks green onions, finely chopped
- ½ cup frozen peas and carrots (optional)
- 2 tablespoons soy sauce
- Kosher salt (optional)

Fried rice often is considered a side dish. But we prefer to treat it as the main feature. It is incredibly flexible, given that you can use just about any variety of rice and any mix of ingredients. The key is to use cold cooked rice, which doesn't have as much moisture and potential to result in soggy fried rice. You certainly could use fresh rice, if that's what you have; it'll still be delicious, even if the texture is softer. If you've never tried fried brown rice, I highly recommend it for the wonderful aroma and just-right chew. This is a basic recipe that you can customize to your taste. Serve with hot sauce, curry, extra onions, shallots, different kinds of greens, or cilantro. See options for proteins on the following page.

■ Fluff the rice by breaking up any big pieces with your fingers or a fork. You need to loosen up the grains, especially if using short- or medium-grain rice, which tends to be stickier. This will make it easier to stir-fry.

■ Preheat a wok over medium heat until wisps of smoke rise from the surface. Add 1 tablespoon of the oil and heat until it starts to shimmer. Add the eggs, which will quickly pool at the bottom. Cook the eggs for a few seconds, then start to scramble them. When the eggs are soft-cooked, not hard, turn off the heat, transfer the eggs to a small bowl, and set aside. Rinse the wok and dry with a towel.

■ Return the wok to the stove over high heat. Add the remaining 1 tablespoon oil, immediately add the onions, and fry for about 5 seconds, or until softened. Add the eggs and stir for about 5 seconds or so to break up the pieces. Add the rice and peas and carrots, then reduce the heat to medium. Using a spatula, scoop, stir, and flip the rice to combine it with the vegetables. Break apart any remaining large chunks of rice. Add the soy sauce. Actively stir and scoop the rice to help it heat through and to prevent it from burning. If needed, add salt to taste.

→

FRIED RICE PROTEIN OPTIONS

Chicken Cut 2 boneless chicken thighs into roughly ¾-inch dice. Mix in 2 teaspoons soy sauce. Brown the chicken in about 1 tablespoon of vegetable oil. Add the chicken to the fried rice when you add the rice.

Beef Thinly slice about 4 ounces of beef against the grain. The cut isn't so important if you make the slices very thin. Mix in 2 teaspoons soy sauce. Brown the beef in about 1 tablespoon of vegetable oil. Add the beef to the fried rice when you add the rice.

Chinese sausage Slice 2 to 3 links of your favorite brand of Chinese sausage into ¼-inch pieces. In a small skillet over medium heat, brown the sausage pieces on each side for 1 to 2 minutes. Remove the sausage to a paper towel–lined plate to drain. You can reserve the rendered fat to cook the green onions. Add the sausage to the fried rice when you add the rice.

Chinese barbecued pork Buy about ¼ to ⅓ pound of barbecued pork, or make your own (see page 239), and cut it into ½-inch dice. Add the pork to the fried rice when you add the rice.

Shrimp Cook about 1 cup of bay shrimp in 1 tablespoon of vegetable oil just until the shrimp turn pink. Add the shrimp to the fried rice when you add the rice.

咖哩素菜炒飯

Vegetable Fried Rice

with Curry

MAKES 4 SERVINGS

- 5 cups cold cooked rice
- 2 tablespoons vegetable oil, divided
- 2 eggs, beaten
- 2 stalks green onions, finely chopped
- 1 cup broccoli florets, cut into bite-size pieces and blanched for 1 minute
- 1 cup thinly sliced napa cabbage or other leafy greens
- 3 to 4 shiitake mushrooms, sliced
- 1 tablespoon soy sauce
- 2 teaspoons curry powder
- ½ teaspoon kosher salt, plus more as needed
- Chili paste (optional)

When you're in the restaurant business, your meal times are never normal. Growing up, we couldn't eat lunch until after the lunch shift at two thirty, and we'd always have dinner at ten or ten thirty at night. While we tried to sit down at the table as a family, it wasn't always possible. On those occasions when I had lunch on my own, my mother would make me this vegetable fried rice with curry (my brothers didn't care for it). At the restaurant, where the wok ranges hit more than one hundred and fifty thousand Btus, the searing heat would impart that telltale wok flavor into the fried rice. The succulence of the vegetables, the char of the rice, and the spice of the curry melded perfectly. I have only a fraction of the Btus at home, so it's hard to achieve the same level of wok flavor. But every bite still takes me down memory lane.

▪ Fluff the rice by breaking up any big pieces with your fingers or a fork. You need to loosen up the grains, especially if you have short- or medium-grain rice, which tends to be stickier. This will make it easier to stir-fry.

▪ Preheat a wok over high heat until wisps of smoke rise from the surface. Add 1 tablespoon of the oil and heat until it starts to shimmer. Add the eggs, which will quickly pool at the bottom. Reduce the heat to medium. Let the eggs cook for a few more seconds and then start to scramble them. When the eggs are soft-cooked, not hard, turn off the heat, transfer the eggs to a small bowl, and set aside. Rinse the wok and dry with a towel.

▪ Return the wok to the stove over high heat. Add the remaining 1 tablespoon oil, immediately add the onions, and fry for about 5 seconds, or until softened. Add the broccoli, cabbage, and mushrooms, and stir vigorously to combine. Continue to stir-fry for 1 to 2 minutes, or until the cabbage has softened a bit. Add the eggs and stir to combine.

▪ Add the rice. Reduce the heat to medium. Using a spatula, scoop, stir, and flip the rice to combine it with the vegetables. Break apart any remaining large chunks of rice. You have to actively stir and scoop the rice to help it heat through and prevent it from burning. Add the soy sauce, curry powder, and salt, and stir well to combine. Taste for seasoning. Add additional salt to taste, if needed. Add chili paste to taste. Stir well again, and serve.

稀飯

Simple Congee

MAKES 4 SERVINGS

2 cups cooked rice, or 1 cup uncooked rice

Condiments of your choice (see below)

Making congee, or rice porridge, is akin to making a sandwich, which can range from a simple peanut butter and jelly between two slices of white bread to an extravagant, perfectly toasted handmade sandwich with crusty bread filled with carefully sourced ingredients and topped with a fried egg. I most often make congee with leftover rice and serve it with an assortment of pickles and savory condiments. Some like it thicker and denser; others like it soupier and less sludge-like. You can use broth instead of water to help flavor the congee. I prefer making a plain congee and then adding various condiments for flavor.

■ If starting with cooked rice, in a pot over medium-high heat, add the rice and cover it with water by ½ inch. Bring to a simmer, then reduce the heat to low and simmer for 20 to 40 minutes, or until thick. The longer you simmer, the more the rice grains expand, break apart, and thicken to a creamy texture. Stir on occasion to keep the rice from sticking to the bottom of the pot.

■ If starting with uncooked rice, in a pot over medium-high heat, add the uncooked rice and 4 cups water. Bring to a boil, then reduce the heat to low and simmer, stirring frequently, for about 1 hour, or until thick. If you like a creamier texture, then let the rice simmer for up to 1½ hours.

CONGEE CONDIMENTS

Century eggs I keep a package of these preserved duck eggs in my refrigerator. They're usually sold in packs of four or six. I prefer the eggs with the soft center. Others may prefer the eggs with the hard center. To serve, peel and cut the eggs into four wedges. Drizzle with soy sauce, sesame oil, and minced cilantro if desired.

Chinese sausage Slice 2 to 3 links of your favorite brand of Chinese sausage into ¼-inch pieces. Render the sausage to heat through and release the fat. Remove the rendered sausage to a paper towel to drain before serving.

Spicy peanuts Some Asian markets carry Huang Fei Hong Spicy Peanuts, which are seasoned with red chili peppers and Sichuan peppercorns. You can also buy them online. They are an addictive snack and pair nicely with congee.

Simple Stir-Fried Greens (page 137)

Tomato Egg (page 141)

Pickles There are many varieties of pickled radishes or cucumbers that you can buy at an Asian market to try with your congee.

Canned eel You can buy Chinese-style eel in a tin. It comes roasted with or without fermented black beans.

Smacked Cucumber (page 82)

Just a Roasted Sweet Potato (page 81)

擔仔麵

Shrimp and Pork Noodles in Broth

(Dan Zi Mian)

MAKES 4 SERVINGS

- ½ pound shell-on, medium or large raw Gulf shrimp
- 1½ quarts Chicken Broth (page 173)
- ¾ pound dried Chinese noodles
- 1 tablespoon vegetable oil
- ½ pound ground pork
- 2 teaspoons finely minced garlic
- 2 stalks green onions, cut into 2-inch segments
- ½ cup water
- 2 tablespoons soy sauce
- 2 teaspoons Chinese black vinegar or balsamic vinegar
- 1½ cups bean sprouts

This noodle soup was invented by Taiwanese fishermen in the late 1800s. During the off season, the fishermen would carry the noodles on a shoulder pole and sell them on the streets. My mother used to make this dish for my father. She didn't use chicken broth but made a quick broth from the shrimp. But she also had the benefit of a commercial wok, so the high-heat searing of the ingredients imparted its special flavor. This is a simplified version. You also can try the more traditional version made with Lu Rou (see note).

- Peel and devein the shrimp, and reserve the shells. Set the shrimp aside.

- In a 4-quart pot over medium heat, add the shells and the chicken broth, and simmer for about 30 minutes to infuse the broth with shrimp flavor.

- In the meantime, cook the noodles according to the package's instructions.

- Strain the broth to remove the shells, reserving the broth. Return the broth to the pot and keep warm over low heat. Add the peeled shrimp, and poach for about 10 minutes.

- Preheat a wok over high heat until wisps of smoke rise from the surface. Add the oil and heat until it starts to shimmer. Add the ground pork and, using a spatula, break it up to help the meat brown. Add the garlic and onions, and stir-fry for a few seconds to combine. Add the water, soy sauce, and vinegar, and stir to combine. Reduce the heat to low and simmer for 5 minutes more, or until the sauce has reduced and is nearly dry. Turn off the heat.

- Divide the cooked noodles between four bowls. Spoon some of the pork on each mound of noodles, then add 3 to 4 shrimp and bean sprouts to each. Ladle the broth over the noodles. Serve immediately.

NOTE: For the Lu Rou variation, see page 188. Substitute the Lu Rou for the pork and serve with halved Marbled Soy Sauce Eggs (page 85).

粉蒸排骨

Steamed Spare Ribs

with Rice Powder

MAKES 4 SERVINGS

- 1½ pounds "sweet-and-sour" cut pork spare ribs
- 3 tablespoons soy sauce
- 2 tablespoons Shaoxing wine or dry Marsala wine
- 2 tablespoons water
- 1 teaspoon minced fresh ginger
- 2 stalks green onions, cut into 2-inch segments
- 2 cloves garlic, crushed or minced
- 1 medium sweet potato, peeled and sliced into ½-inch-thick rounds
- 1 packet (about 2 ounces) rice powder (see note)
- Simple Stir-Fried Greens (page 137), for serving (optional)

We call this dish *fen zheng pai gu* (*fen*, or "rice powder," *zheng*, or "steam," and *pai gu*, or "ribs"). We didn't have this often, so when we did, it felt special. You marinate the ribs, coat them with five-spice-flavored rice powder, which is more granules than a powder, and then steam them to intensify the flavor and cook the rice. To me, it's the perfect bite, because you get the savory, meaty ribs and rice all at once. You also can use thick-sliced pork belly or beef, and steam it atop thick slices of sweet potatoes, which benefit from the rendered meat juices during the steaming process. Look for "sweet-and-sour" cut pork ribs, which are readily available at Asian markets, or ask your local butcher to cut the ribs for you.

▪ Cut the spare ribs into segments, cutting between the bones. In a large bowl, combine the soy sauce, wine, water, ginger, onions, and garlic. Add the ribs and stir to coat. Cover the bowl and place in the refrigerator. Marinate for at least 30 minutes and up to overnight.

▪ Set up a steamer (see page 47) with enough water to steam the ribs for at least 1 hour, or check the water level during the cooking process and add water as needed. Place the sweet potatoes in a steam-proof dish, such as a pie plate. Drain the ribs. In the same bowl, add the rice powder to the ribs and mix well to coat. Place the marinated ribs on the layer of sweet potatoes and then steam for at least 1 hour and 10 minutes. Check the ribs for tenderness. If they're not tender enough, steam for 10 to 15 minutes more and check again. Repeat as needed. Serve immediately with some stir-fried greens on the side, if desired.

NOTE: There are different brands of rice or steam powder, and the boxes may not be decipherable. You may have to ask for help to find it at an Asian market. You will have better luck at a Chinese market. Alternatively, you can make your own: In a dry skillet over medium-low heat, toast ½ cup long-grain rice (such as jasmine) for about 10 minutes, stirring continuously. After it's done toasting, set the rice aside to cool. Use a spice grinder to grind the rice into sesame-seed-size pellets. You do not want it to be a fine powder. After you have roughly ground the rice, add ½ teaspoon five-spice powder and mix well.

炸醬麵

Chinese Noodles in Meat Sauce

(Zha Jiang Mian)

MAKES 4 TO 6 SERVINGS

For the sauce:

4 tablespoons vegetable oil, divided

1 pound ground pork

1 cup diced fresh tomatoes

1 stalk green onion, finely chopped

2 teaspoons finely minced garlic

1 teaspoon finely minced fresh ginger

1½ cup water

3 tablespoons soy sauce

3 tablespoons sweet bean sauce

1 tablespoon bean sauce

1 tablespoon Shaoxing wine or dry Marsala wine

1 teaspoon sugar

1 cup frozen peas and carrots (optional)

1 pound dried thin or wide Chinese noodles

1 cucumber or 2 Persian cucumbers, finely julienned, for garnish

2 stalks green onions, finely chopped, for garnish

Chili sauce, for garnish

My husband and kids call this "Chinese spaghetti" because the Chinese name is hard for them to pronounce. *Zha jian mian* literally translates to "fried sauce noodles." It indeed resembles an Italian ragu or meat sauce. This dish is usually made with minced beef or pork and may include any number of diced vegetables, including carrots, napa cabbage, and shiitake mushrooms. My mom always used ground pork and frozen peas and carrots—which we always had around for the fried rice we served at the restaurant. I've tried adding shiitake mushrooms and pressed tofu (*tofu gan*) to the sauce, but the kids (my husband included) prefer the peas-and-carrots version.

■ Bring a large pot of water to a boil over high heat.

■ Meanwhile, make the sauce. Preheat a wok over high heat until wisps of smoke rise from the surface. Add 3 tablespoons of the oil and heat until it starts to shimmer. Carefully add the ground pork, breaking it up with your spatula. You want the meat to fry in the oil and get some crispy edges. Break up, stir, and flip the pork bits to get all sides. Once browned with some crispy edges, remove the wok from the heat. Using a slotted spoon, transfer the pork to a small bowl and set aside. Discard any residual oil and rendered fat. There's no need to wash the wok, but you can wipe the surface with a kitchen towel or clean sponge.

■ Return the wok to the stove over high heat, add the remaining 1 tablespoon oil, and heat until it starts to shimmer. Add the tomatoes, onions, garlic, and ginger. Stir-fry for 1 to 2 minutes, or until the tomatoes have cooked down slightly. Add the water, soy sauce, sweet bean sauce, bean sauce, wine, and sugar, and stir again to combine. Let simmer for 2 minutes. Add the browned pork and stir to combine. Add the peas and carrots, and stir to combine. Reduce the heat to low and let the sauce simmer, stirring frequently, for about 10 minutes more, or until the sauce has thickened slightly.

■ While the sauce is simmering, add the noodles to the boiling water, and cook for 9 to 11 minutes, or until the noodles are soft, not mushy, and still have structure. The cooking time will depend on the type of noodle. Drain.

■ To serve, toss the noodles in the sauce, or arrange the noodles on a plate and ladle the sauce on top. Garnish with the cucumber, onions, and chili sauce.

蝦仁蔬菜炒麵

Stir-Fried Noodles

with Shrimp and Vegetables

MAKES 4 SERVINGS

¾ pound dried Chinese noodles

½ pound raw shrimp, peeled and deveined

1 teaspoon soy sauce

2 teaspoons cornstarch

For the sauce:

½ cup water

2 tablespoons soy sauce

1 teaspoon minced fresh ginger

1 stalk green onion, finely chopped

1 large clove garlic, minced

1 tablespoon plus 1 teaspoon vegetable oil, divided

1 stalk green onion, cut into 2-inch segments

½ medium carrot, julienned (about ½ cup)

3 to 4 cups roughly chopped greens, such as baby bok choy, yu choy, or Chinese broccoli

½ teaspoon sesame oil

Kosher salt (optional)

This recipe can wear many different hats because you can change the protein and vegetables according to what you have on hand. Since my kids have opposite food aversions, I sometimes make the noodles and sauce first, then stir-fry the protein and vegetables separately so that I can layer them on the noodles strategically. This way, no one has to spend the first few minutes picking stuff out. That said, presenting the vegetables and meat atop a mound of noodles does create a lovely visual.

■ Bring a large pot of water to boil over high heat. It's not necessary to salt the water, since the sauce is quite savory. Add the noodles and cook for 9 to 11 minutes, or until the noodles are soft but not mushy on the outside, and have a little chew on the inside. The cooking time will depend on the thickness of the noodles.

■ In a small bowl, put the shrimp and the soy sauce, and mix well. Add the cornstarch and mix well again. Set aside.

■ To make the sauce, in a small bowl, put the water, soy sauce, ginger, onions, and garlic, and stir to combine. Set aside.

■ Drain the noodles and set aside. If you are not using the noodles within 5 minutes, to prevent sticking, add 1 tablespoon oil to the noodles and incorporate with tongs.

■ Preheat a wok over high heat until wisps of smoke rise from the surface. Add 1 tablespoon of the vegetable oil and heat until it starts to shimmer. Add the shrimp in a single layer to the bowl of the wok and sear for 30 to 40 seconds, or until the shrimp have begun to turn pink. Flip the shrimp and sear for 30 to 40 seconds more. Remove the pan from the heat, transfer the shrimp to a small bowl, and set aside. If there are any charred bits in the wok, gently scrape them out.

■ Return the wok to the stove over high heat. Add the remaining 1 teaspoon vegetable oil, immediately add the onions, and stir for about 5 seconds to release the aroma. Add the carrots and stir for a few seconds. Add the greens and continue stirring and scooping to mix for about 1 minute. Add the shrimp and the sauce, and stir again to combine. Add the noodles and carefully stir and scoop to mix. It may be helpful to use tongs. Once well combined, drizzle on the sesame oil. Remove the wok from the heat. Add a dash more soy sauce or salt to taste. Serve.

牛肉炒河粉

Stir-Fried Fresh Rice Noodles

(Chow Fun) with Beef

MAKES 4 SERVINGS

½ pound flank steak

3 tablespoons plus 1 teaspoon soy sauce, divided

1 teaspoon cornstarch

2 tablespoons vegetable oil, divided

1 pound fresh rice noodles, presliced

2 cups roughly chopped *gai lan*

½ medium carrot, peeled and julienned (about ½ cup)

½ cup bean sprouts

1 cup water

1 tablespoon hoisin sauce

Kosher salt

You probably have tasted stir-fried *chow fun* noodles at a dim sum restaurant. These fresh rice noodles are made in sheets that can then be filled to make rice noodle rolls or cut into various widths for stir-fries. This dish is best with freshly made rice noodles. Well-stocked Asian markets usually offer locally made *chow fun* noodles that are so fresh, the package may still be warm. Once the noodles get refrigerated, they harden and become difficult to cook. Unfurl the noodles before you start cooking. While this recipe uses *gai lan*, you can use any leafy greens you choose, including yu choy and Chinese broccoli.

■ Trim the flank steak of any large pieces of membrane. Cut the flank in half or thirds lengthwise, or with the grain. Depending on the total width of the flank, you may get two or three sections that are about 2½ inches wide. Cut these sections against the grain into ⅛-inch slices. Put the sliced beef in a medium bowl. Add 1 tablespoon plus 1 teaspoon of the soy sauce and mix well. Add the cornstarch and mix well again. Set aside.

■ Preheat a wok over high heat until wisps of smoke rise from the surface. Add 1 tablespoon of the oil and heat until it starts to shimmer. Gently add the beef in a single layer. Sear for about 1 minute, then stir-fry the beef, breaking up any pieces that have stuck together. Remove the pan from the heat and transfer the beef to a medium bowl. Rinse the wok and dry with a towel.

■ Separate the noodles and set aside.

■ Return the wok to the stove and heat over high heat until wisps of smoke rise from the surface. Add the remaining 1 tablespoon oil and heat until it starts to shimmer. Add the *gai lan*, carrots, and bean sprouts, and stir-fry for 1 minute, or until soft. Add the water, the remaining 2 tablespoons soy sauce, and the hoisin, and stir to combine. Add salt to taste. (The sauce needs to be slightly overseasoned to accommodate the noodles.) Add the noodles and stir-fry gently, but quickly and thoroughly, until all the noodles have been coated with sauce, about 2 to 3 minutes. Serve immediately.

紅燒牛肉麵

Red-Braised Beef Noodle Soup

MAKES 4 SERVINGS

- About 2 pounds of boneless beef shin shank, or 2 to 2½ pounds bone-in, cross-cut (for osso buco) beef shank (see note, opposite page)
- 20 cups water, divided
- 2 tablespoons vegetable oil
- 3 stalks green onions, cut into three segments
- 4 to 6 large cloves garlic, lightly smashed
- 3 large slices fresh ginger, cut on the bias (about 3 inches long and ¼ inch thick)
- ½ cup Shaoxing wine or dry Marsala wine
- ½ cup soy sauce
- 3 tablespoons bean sauce
- 1 tablespoon rock sugar or light brown sugar
- ½ teaspoon whole Sichuan peppercorns
- 2 dried red chili peppers
- 1 star anise
- Kosher salt (optional)

This dish is the epitome of Chinese soul food for me. It's rich, soothing, and restorative. It is common enough to be considered "street food" and perfected enough to inspire a cult following. I eat this soup frequently enough that my kids are now just as enthusiastic about it. They know by the aroma of beef shank simmering with green onions, garlic, star anise, and soy sauce that I'm making red-braised beef noodle soup. I fantasize about eating my way across Taipei at all the well-known beef noodle soup shops. When I cook this at home and I have time to go the extra mile, I will make hand-cut noodles. The hearty texture of shaved or handmade noodles ups the comfort quotient.

▪ If using boneless shin shank, it will be one long piece of muscle that's tapered at both ends and wide in the center. It will be covered in membrane, and maybe some small pieces of fat. You can trim this off with a sharp boning knife. Cut the shank crosswise into three to four sections. In a stockpot or Dutch oven, add the meat and 6 cups of the water. Bring to a boil over high heat, reduce the heat to medium, and simmer for 5 minutes, or until some of the scum has floated to the top. Remove the pot from the heat and transfer the beef to a large bowl. This process rids the meat of some of the scum and blood. Discard the liquid. Rinse and dry the pot, and return to the stove.

▪ Cut the beef into chunks that are roughly 2 inches across. Be careful of any tendons that may be at the ends, because they are still tough and will resist the knife. If you have bone-in shank, cut 2-inch chunks from around the bone, reserving the bone for the broth. Set aside.

▪ Return the pot to the stove over high heat. Add the oil, onions, garlic, and ginger, and fry the aromatics, stirring well, for about 30 seconds. Add the beef chunks and stir to combine. Add the wine, soy sauce, bean sauce, sugar, peppercorns, chili peppers, and star anise, and stir to combine. Let the liquid come to a slow boil. If you used a bone-in cut and reserved the bones, add them to the pot. Top with 12 cups of the water and bring to a boil. Reduce the heat to low and simmer for 1 hour, occasionally skimming off any scum from the surface. Add the remaining 2 cups water and continue to simmer for 30 to 40 minutes, or until the largest chunks of beef are tender to the bite. Skim off any

1 batch Home-Style Hand-Cut Noodles (recipe follows), or 1 pound Chinese noodles

2 small heads baby bok choy, leaves separated

½ cup roughly chopped fresh cilantro, for garnish

3 stalks finely chopped green onions, for garnish

½ cup finely diced Pickled Chinese Mustard Greens (page 157) or store-bought, for garnish

Chili sauce (optional), for serving

Tip: Use a disposable tea filter bag for the spices so that you don't have to strain the broth. You simply can fish out the bag of spices when you're done cooking. Look for the tea bags online or at Asian markets. Daiso is also a good source. A pack of a hundred tea filters costs five or six dollars.

remaining scum or pools of oil. Taste the broth as you go and notice how the flavor gradually becomes more concentrated. Add salt to taste. Remove the pot from the heat.

▪ If you don't mind bits of spices in your soup, skip this step. Using a slotted spoon or tongs, remove the beef from the broth and set aside. Carefully pour the broth through a fine-mesh sieve into a large heatproof bowl or container. You should have about 8 to 10 cups broth remaining. Return the beef to the pot and top with the strained broth. If necessary, you can refrigerate the broth for 1 day. Otherwise, keep the broth warm over low heat while you prepare the noodles.

▪ Bring a second pot of water to a boil over high heat, and cook the hand-cut noodles according to the recipe that follows. If using Chinese noodles, cook according to the package's instructions.

▪ Add the bok choy leaves to the broth about 10 minutes before you're ready to serve.

▪ Drain the noodles, and distribute them evenly between four bowls, leaving about 1 inch headspace from the rim. Add 2 to 3 chunks of beef and some bok choy to each bowl, as desired, and then ladle the broth over the noodles.

▪ Garnish the bowls with the cilantro, onions, and greens, and serve with chili sauce on the side.

NOTE: You can find boneless beef shank at Asian markets. Retail cuts are generally about 10 to 12 inches in length, tapered at the ends, and roughly 4½ to 5 inches at the widest point. This is the shin muscle. It is usually covered partially in silver skin, which you can trim off.

Home-Style Hand-Cut Noodles

MAKES 1 POUND

1 batch Dumpling Dough (page 67)

All-purpose flour, for dusting

We never really measured when we made dumplings, so there was usually leftover dough; it would be just enough to roll a couple of green onion pancakes or make some hand-cut noodles. My mother used to make noodles for my father, usually in a bowl of quick soup, and he would slurp up the noodles with such glee and appreciation that I came to expect his post-meal refrain about how much he preferred hand-cut noodles to store-bought. My kids now prefer homemade noodles too, especially when I serve them in the red-braised beef broth.

→

- Make the dough according to the recipe. While the dough is resting, line a baking sheet with parchment paper. Set aside.

- Once rested, knead the dough by hand for about 2 minutes, or until smooth. Divide the dough into four sections and work with one section at a time. Shape each piece of dough roughly into a rectangle. (If you start with a rectangular shape, you are more likely to roll out a rectangular sheet.)

- Generously dust your work surface with flour. Roll out one piece of dough, trying your best to maintain the rectangular shape, until it is about ⅛ inch thick. It will be slightly thinner than a store-bought flour tortilla, and 18 to 22 inches long by 7 to 8 inches wide. Dust your work surface and the dough with flour as you go to keep the dough from sticking to the rolling pin.

- Trim any stray edges from the rolled-out dough so that you have relatively even sides. Dust the dough generously and fold the rectangle in half lengthwise, so that you join short edge to short edge. Fold that in half again. Turn the folded dough so that the folds are facing you. Using a sharp knife, cut noodles that are about ¼ inch in width. Dust the cut noodles with flour and use your hands to unfurl the noodles. Place the bundle of noodles on the prepared baking sheet. Repeat with the remaining portions of dough.

- In a large pot over high heat, bring about 4 quarts of water to a boil. Set 1 cup of cold tap water on the counter next to the stove.

- Drop the noodles into the pot in batches. Stir immediately to keep the noodles from clumping. The noodles will take about 3 to 5 minutes to cook, so don't walk away. When the water begins to bubble up, add about ½ cup of the cold water to keep it at a manageable simmer. Add additional cold water as needed. Test a noodle. It should be cooked through but still have a tiny bit of chew. Drain and use immediately.

- If you aren't using the noodles immediately, you can "shock" them under running cold tap water to cool them off and keep them from becoming a giant noodle brick. When ready to serve, dip the noodles in hot, simmering water for about 1 minute to bring them back to temperature.

NOTE: After you cut the noodles, you can freeze them to use later. Place the noodles in small bundles on a parchment-lined baking sheet, freeze them for about 1 hour, then transfer the bundles to a ziplock bag to finish freezing. When ready to cook, do not defrost the noodles. Drop the frozen bundles into boiling water and cook for 4 to 6 minutes.

小炒

Stir-Fries

Even when there's "nothing" in the refrigerator and I'm running behind schedule, I always can find some combination of vegetables, aromatics, and a small amount of protein to stir-fry quickly and serve with steamed rice. This means I never worry about putting dinner on the table for my family. Armed with the basic principles behind everyday stir-fries and some practice with the recipes here, you soon will be just as capable of improvising ingredient combinations. I encourage you to experiment, because the beauty of a stir-fry is that it can bend to whatever ingredients you have on hand and to your particular stove and pan situation. Certainly, using a wok is ideal. But if you don't have a wok yet, don't let that stop you from making a skillet stir-fry. To be clear, I'm not saying that a skillet is a good substitute for a wok when it comes to stir-frying; I simply want to empower people to get into the kitchen.

When I teach classes on stir-frying, my favorite aha moment to witness is when a student finishes making a straightforward dish, such as Baby Bok Choy with Chicken, and then takes the first bite. Universally, the response is: "I had no idea it was that easy and so delicious." My reply is always a reminder: "And *you* made it." Seeing the light in people's eyes is my reward.

The subject of stir-frying inevitably triggers a comment—or complaint—about all the cutting and prep work involved in Chinese cooking. Here is where Asian and many Western cuisines diverge. Stir-frying is a high-heat, quick-cooking method that necessitates ingredients to be cut uniformly into bite-size pieces so they then can be eaten with chopsticks. I will slice up flank steak to cook with asparagus segments and soy sauce for a stir-fry. On another night, when I'm not cooking Chinese dishes, I may take that same flank steak with asparagus, season them with olive oil, salt, and pepper, and then grill them whole. Then I have to set the table with knives and forks. Cutting is still necessary; it just takes place after cooking.

Most of the recipes in this chapter offer room for improvisation. Love garlic? Add some. Don't have bok choy but your garden is overgrown with kale? Use the kale. Need to make a gluten-free version? Use salt instead of soy sauce—or a gluten-free soy sauce. Unlike baking, stir-frying is laid-back. Let the recipes inspire you as you build your own repertoire.

雞絲炒青江菜

Baby Bok Choy

with Chicken

MAKES 4 SERVINGS

- 8 ounces chicken breast, about 1 cup
- 2 tablespoons soy sauce, divided
- 2 teaspoons cornstarch
- 3 tablespoons vegetable oil, divided
- 3 to 4 heads baby bok choy, trimmed and leaves separated
- ¼ cup water
- 1 large clove garlic, crushed
- Kosher salt
- ¼ teaspoon sesame oil

Suggested pairing: Beef with Broccoli (page 234).

When I taught this dish in a cooking class, the response was resoundingly positive. Students were surprised by how straightforward it was to prepare and by how much flavor just a few ingredients could yield. Until that point, I had thought such a simple stir-fry would be too boring for students to make. It was a reminder that what's second nature to me isn't necessarily so for my students. This recipe is a basic formula that you can apply to any number of proteins, vegetables, and aromatics. A note on bok choy: One head of baby bok choy can range in size from as small as three to four inches long and about one and a half inches in diameter to more than six inches long and three inches wide. If the heads are small, then I may trim and separate the leaves but not cut them. If the heads are large, then I will separate the leaves and slice them crosswise into half-inch-wide slices.

- Cut the chicken breast lengthwise into two to three strips, about 1½ inches wide, or about the size of chicken tenders. Then slice each strip of chicken crosswise into slivers. The exact size of the slivers is not as important as keeping the pieces relatively uniform. In a small bowl, combine the chicken with 1 tablespoon of the soy sauce and mix well. Add the cornstarch and mix well again.

- Preheat a wok over high heat until wisps of smoke rise from the surface. Add 2 tablespoons of the vegetable oil and heat until it shimmers. Add the chicken and, using a spatula, quickly spread it into a single layer in the bowl of the wok. After about 15 seconds, stir-fry the chicken for about 1 more minute, or until the chicken is nearly cooked through. Remove the wok from the heat, transfer the chicken into a small bowl, and set aside. Rinse the wok and dry with a towel.

- Return the wok to the stove over high heat. Add the remaining 1 tablespoon vegetable oil and heat until it starts to shimmer.

- Add the bok choy leaves and stir for about 1 minute. The leaves will begin to wilt and turn dark green. Add the chicken and stir-fry for a few seconds to combine. Add the remaining 1 tablespoon soy sauce and the water and garlic, and stir until all the bok choy leaves and chicken are just cooked through, 1 to 2 minutes. Add salt to taste.

- Drizzle with sesame oil, and serve with steamed rice.

簡易炒青菜

Simple Stir-Fried Greens

MAKES 4 SERVINGS

- ¾ pound greens, such as baby bok choy or yu choy, trimmed
- 1 tablespoon vegetable oil
- 2 medium cloves garlic, finely minced
- 2 tablespoons water
- 1 tablespoon soy sauce or 1 teaspoon kosher salt
- ½ teaspoon sesame oil

Suggested pairings: Any other stir-fry dish, especially a meaty one, such as Sweet-and-Sour Spare Ribs (page 193), Red-Braised Pork Belly (page 187), or Three-Cup Chicken (page 152).

When I tell my husband I need to go shopping at one of the Asian markets, he knows it usually means we're out of Chinese greens—or soy sauce or rice. I go at least once a week to stock up on baby bok choy, yu choy, napa cabbage, Chinese mustard greens, and other leafy vegetables. If there is a bounty of vegetables, I need only a pot of rice to make a satisfying meal. You can use your choice of leafy Asian greens in this recipe. Feel free to experiment with other types of greens, such as kale, chard, and escarole.

■ Cut the greens into bite-size pieces. Depending on the vegetable, the dimensions will vary, so use your best judgment. Set aside.

■ Preheat a wok over high heat until wisps of smoke rise from the surface. Add the vegetable oil and garlic and stir for about 5 seconds. Then add the greens and quickly stir-fry to mix with the garlic. The oil and heat will begin to wilt the greens. Continue to stir and toss the greens for 2 to 3 minutes. Add the water and soy sauce. Toss to combine, and stir-fry until the greens have wilted and don't look raw, about 1 to 3 minutes more depending on the type of vegetable. Add the sesame oil and stir to combine. Serve with steamed rice or Simple Congee (page 118).

清炒葱花玉米

Wok-Seared Corn

and Green Onions

MAKES 4 SERVINGS

4 ears fresh corn or 1 (10-ounce) bag frozen corn

1 tablespoon vegetable oil

2 stalks green onions, finely chopped

1 tablespoon soy sauce

1 tablespoon water

Kosher salt

Suggested pairing: Baby Bok Choy with Chicken (page 135).

I usually keep a bag of frozen corn on hand for when I need a quick stir-fry to pair with a meat-centric meal. In my house, corn is also one of the few vegetables that *both* kids will eat. I start by frying chopped green onions in a touch of oil to release their aromatic goodness to counter the sweetness of the corn. I use fresh corn in season when it's abundant and sweet. Fresh corn also chars nicely, which adds a hint of smokiness. While there are different ways to remove the kernels from the cob, I usually lay the cob flat on its side and use a sharp chef's knife to cut off the kernels. You can easily scale this recipe up or down and add other ingredients, such as minced garlic, chili peppers, or fresh cilantro, to taste.

- If using fresh corn, cut the kernels from the cob. Set aside.

- Preheat a wok over high heat until wisps of smoke rise from the surface. Add the oil and onions, and quickly stir to combine for 10 seconds, or until the onions are fragrant.

- Add the corn, and stir-fry for about 1 minute. If you are using frozen corn, it will sizzle as the ice crystals melt and release moisture.

- Add the soy sauce and water, and continue to stir. After 1 to 2 minutes more, the corn should have a light sear and be fully cooked through. Add salt to taste. Serve with steamed rice.

番茄炒蛋

Tomato Egg

MAKES 3 TO 4 SERVINGS

- 2 tablespoons plus 1 teaspoon vegetable oil, divided
- 1 stalk green onion, finely chopped
- 6 large eggs, beaten
- 1 cup diced fresh tomatoes, the juiciest variety you can find
- 2 tablespoons soy sauce
- 1 to 2 tablespoons water
- Chili sauce (optional)
- ¼ teaspoon sesame oil

The brilliance of eggs is undeniable. Out of all the ways to prepare eggs, scrambled is the least exciting to me—probably because they're often overcooked. The exception is tomato eggs. While I was growing up, I remember telling my friends about tomato eggs and getting blank looks in return. It didn't occur to me that having eggs stir-fried with tomatoes and soy sauce wasn't common. Summer tomatoes, of course, make this dish a simple stunner. Even with muted winter tomatoes, this dish is still a winner.

■ Preheat the wok over medium heat until wisps of smoke rise from the surface. Add 2 tablespoons of the vegetable oil and the green onions, and stir-fry for 10 seconds. Add the eggs and cook, gently scrambling the eggs, for about 1 minute, or until the curds have set but aren't hard. Remove the pan from the heat, transfer the eggs to a medium bowl, and set aside. Rinse out the wok and dry with a towel.

■ Return the wok to the stove over high heat. Add the remaining 1 teaspoon vegetable oil and heat until it starts to shimmer. Add the diced tomatoes, and stir-fry until they are soft and have released their juices, about 1 minute. Add the soy sauce and stir-fry for 1 minute.

■ Add the eggs and stir to combine. If it looks too dry, add the water. Add chili sauce to taste. Gently stir-fry for about 1 minute, then drizzle with the sesame oil. Serve with steamed rice or Simple Congee (page 118).

清炒土豆絲

Stir-Fried Shoestring Potatoes

MAKES 4 SERVINGS

- ¾ pound red potatoes, peeled
- 6 ounces meat (pork, chicken, or beef), slivered
- 1½ teaspoons plus 2 tablespoons soy sauce, divided
- 1 teaspoon cornstarch
- 2 tablespoons vegetable oil, divided
- 1 medium carrot, finely julienned
- 1 stalk green onion, finely julienned
- 1 teaspoon rice vinegar
- ¼ teaspoon white pepper powder

Suggested pairings: Beef with Asparagus and Shiitake Mushrooms (page 155) or Five-Spice Tofu Gan with Slivered Pork and Celery (page 161).

Potatoes get pigeonholed to a few workhorse preparations that, while delicious, are usually heavy. This stir-fried potatoes dish is the antidote. Because the potatoes pair well with pork, chicken, or beef, it's quite flexible. You can skip the meat altogether for a vegetarian version. I like the light crunch of the potatoes and the flavor the wok imparts.

■ Fill a large bowl (big enough to accommodate all the potatoes) with cold water. Set aside.

■ Slice the potatoes ⅛ inch thick. Take your time; it is worth the effort to make your slices as uniformly thin as you can. As you make the slices, you can shingle them in place or, if it's easier, stack them three or four slices tall. Cut each stack into thin julienne. The exact dimensions aren't as important as making the potato strips consistently thin. Place the potato strips in the cold water and rinse off some of the starch. Set aside to soak.

■ In a small bowl, put the meat and 1½ teaspoons of the soy sauce, and mix well. Add the cornstarch and mix well again. Preheat a wok over high heat until wisps of smoke rise from the surface. Add 1 tablespoon of the oil and heat until it starts to shimmer. Add the meat and, using a spatula, break up the meat and stir-fry for 1 to 2 minutes, or until it has nearly cooked through. Remove the wok from the heat, transfer the meat to a small bowl, and set aside. Rinse the wok, if needed, and dry with a towel.

■ Strain the potato strips.

■ Return the wok to the stove over high heat and heat until wisps of smoke rise from the surface. Add the remaining 1 tablespoon oil and heat until it starts to shimmer. Add the carrots and onions, and stir-fry until the onions become fragrant. Add the potatoes and stir-fry quickly for a few seconds to combine. Add the meat and stir for a few seconds to combine. Add the remaining 2 tablespoons soy sauce and the vinegar, and stir-fry quickly and vigorously for 3 to 4 minutes to distribute the sauce and to cook through the potatoes, which should retain some of their crunch. Stir in the pepper and serve with steamed rice.

辣味花椰菜炒臘肉

Cauliflower with Country Ham

and Jalapeños

MAKES 4 SERVINGS

1 quart plus 2 tablespoons water, divided

1 small head cauliflower (about 1 pound), trimmed and cut into small florets (about 3½ to 4 loosely packed cups)

2 teaspoons vegetable oil

4 to 5 ounces country ham biscuit slices, cut into 12 to 15 bite-size pieces

1 tablespoon plus 1½ teaspoons soy sauce

1 small jalapeño, sliced

1 teaspoon sugar

Suggested pairing: Simple Stir-Fried Greens (page 137).

Since our restaurant was located in Missouri, we had access to good country ham. We served it stir-fried with broccoli and jalapeños to the delight of our customers, who didn't know their beloved country ham could be interpreted in such a way. For ourselves, we made the dish with cauliflower, which I enjoyed even more. The salty smokiness and meaty texture of the country ham play together so nicely in a stir-fry. It's the kind of dish that makes you eat more rice than you intend. If you live outside of the South, you may have to order country ham online. A smoky, thick-cut bacon can pinch hit. In the restaurant, we blanched the cauliflower in oil, which is cumbersome to do in a home kitchen. I offer an adapted method that minimizes the use of oil.

■ Bring 1 quart of the water to a boil over high heat in a 3- or 4-quart pot. Add the cauliflower florets and blanch for 2 minutes, or until the florets change from opaque white to slightly translucent. Drain the cauliflower, transfer to a medium bowl, and set aside.

■ Preheat a wok over high heat until wisps of smoke rise from the surface. Add the oil and heat until it starts to shimmer. Add the ham slices and stir-fry for about 30 seconds. Add the soy sauce and jalapeño, and stir-fry for a few seconds to combine. Add the remaining 2 tablespoons water and the sugar, and stir again for a few seconds. Add the cauliflower and stir-fry for 1 to 2 minutes more, or until the sauce has penetrated the cauliflower. Serve with steamed rice.

魚香茄子

Garlic Eggplant

MAKES 4 SERVINGS

- 1½ pounds Chinese eggplant
- 3 tablespoons vegetable oil
- ¼ pound ground pork
- 1 to 2 tablespoons minced garlic
- 3 stalks green onions, finely chopped
- 1 teaspoon minced fresh ginger
- 3 tablespoons soy sauce
- 2 tablespoons water
- 1 teaspoon chili sauce
- 1 teaspoon rice vinegar or balsamic vinegar
- 1 teaspoon sugar
- ¼ teaspoon sesame oil
- 2 tablespoons chopped fresh cilantro (optional)

Suggested pairings: Dry-Fried Green Beans (page 147) and Ma Po Tofu (page 148).

This dish can go in any number of directions depending on the ingredients. Normally, I brown a little bit of ground pork to flavor the eggplant. I've also used good bacon or some diced Chinese sausage. Often, I'll make it without any meat at all. I like using the long, thin Chinese eggplant, but this recipe works just fine with the standard eggplant you find in your grocery store. Adjust the amount of chili sauce and garlic according to how pungent you like it. Sometimes, I'll add a splash of rice vinegar to get some hot-and-sour action. At the restaurant, we used to flash-fry the eggplant, which isn't practical for a home kitchen. I find that roasting the eggplant in the oven minimizes the amount of oil you have to use. Alternatively, you can steam the eggplant for about fifteen minutes.

- Preheat the oven to 400 degrees F.

- Cut the stem and tail ends off the eggplants. The skin on Chinese eggplants is usually thin, so you don't have to peel them. Cut the eggplant into segments about 3 inches long and about ½ inch thick. Spread the pieces on a baking sheet and roast for 7 to 10 minutes, or until soft.

- Meanwhile, preheat the wok over high heat until wisps of smoke rise from the surface. Add 1 tablespoon of the vegetable oil and heat until it starts to shimmer. Add the pork and, using a spatula, break it up and stir-fry for about 1 minute, or until brown and nearly cooked through. It's okay if the pork gets slightly crispy edges. Remove the wok from the heat, transfer the pork to a small bowl, and set aside. There will be some residual grease and charred bits left in the wok. Rinse the wok and dry with a towel.

- When the eggplant is done roasting, you are ready to stir-fry. Return the wok to the stove over high heat. Add the remaining 2 tablespoons vegetable oil, the garlic, onions, and ginger. Quickly stir the aromatics for about 10 seconds. Add the pork, soy sauce, water, chili sauce, vinegar, and sugar, and stir for a few seconds to combine. Add the eggplant, and toss it in the sauce. Continue to stir-fry for 1 to 2 minutes more, or until the eggplant has absorbed the sauce. Drizzle with sesame oil, toss one last time, and remove the wok from the heat. Sprinkle the cilantro over the top and serve with steamed rice.

乾煸四季豆

Dry-Fried Green Beans

MAKES 4 SERVINGS

¾ pound green beans (haricots verts or regular)

⅓ cup plus 1 tablespoon vegetable oil, divided

4 ounces unseasoned ground pork or ground beef (about ¼ cup)

1 stalk green onion, finely chopped

1 tablespoon minced fresh ginger

1 large clove garlic, finely minced

2 tablespoons soy sauce, plus more as needed

1 tablespoon water

1½ teaspoons sugar

Suggested pairings: Wok-Seared Corn and Green Onions (page 138) or any dish you feel like making. (I have even served these green beans at Thanksgiving with turkey.)

A former coworker once scoffed at the idea that my dry-fried green beans could beat his broccoli salad at an office potluck party. Let's just say that I left the office with an empty dish, and he didn't. This recipe is Sichuanese in origin and involves blistering the green beans using a shallow frying method called *gan bian*, or "dry-frying." *Ya cai*, the fermented stems of a type of Chinese mustard green, is traditionally used to season the beans. I omit this ingredient because it's not widely available and because what is available isn't always the best quality. You can leave out the pork to make this dish vegetarian.

■ Trim the green beans and cut them in half. Line a baking sheet with a few layers of paper towels. Set aside.

■ Preheat a wok over medium-high heat until wisps of smoke rise from the surface. Add ⅓ cup of the oil and heat for 30 to 60 seconds, or until it starts to shimmer. In batches, add the beans to the oil in a single layer. Quickly stir-fry the beans, gently swishing them around in the oil. The skins of the beans will start to blister. Once you see that most of the beans look lightly wrinkled but not necessarily browned, about 1 to 2 minutes, using a slotted spoon, transfer the beans to the prepared paper towel–lined baking sheet to absorb the residual oil. Repeat with the remaining beans. Use a wad of paper towels to absorb any residual oil in the wok and brush away any charred pieces.

■ Return the wok to the stove over high heat, and add the remaining 1 tablespoon oil. Add the pork and, using a spatula, break up the pork. Stir-fry for 1 to 2 minutes, or until brown and cooked through. Add the onions, ginger, and garlic, and stir and toss for a few seconds to combine. Add the soy sauce, water, and sugar, and stir to combine.

■ Add the beans, and stir and toss for a few seconds to combine. If it doesn't taste salty enough, add an additional splash of soy sauce, and stir to incorporate. Serve with steamed rice.

麻婆豆腐

Ma Po Tofu

MAKES 4 SERVINGS

- 1 package of medium-firm or soft (not silken) tofu (about 1 pound)
- 2 cups plus 3 tablespoons water, divided
- 1 teaspoon kosher salt, plus more as needed
- 2 tablespoons cornstarch
- 2 tablespoons vegetable oil
- 2 stalks green onions, finely chopped
- 2 teaspoons minced fresh ginger
- 2 cloves garlic, crushed
- ¾ cup unseasoned ground pork (about 4 ounces), browned
- 1 to 2 tablespoons chili bean sauce (see note)
- 1 teaspoon freshly ground Sichuan peppercorns
- ¼ teaspoon sesame oil
- 1 to 2 tablespoons Chili Oil (page 99), for serving

Suggested pairings: Dry-Fried Green Beans (page 147) and Garlic Eggplant (page 144).

When I go to a Chinese restaurant, especially one that specializes in Sichuanese dishes, I always order ma po tofu and hope that the chef doesn't stray off the path by adding peas and carrots, for example, or using so much soy sauce that the dish is brown instead of chili-paste red. The dish combines tender tofu with an incendiary sauce and some ground beef or pork. I always hope that the sauce has enough Sichuan peppercorn to give it just the right amount of numbing spice—the namesake *ma la*. The most authentic ma po tofu has a dense layer of chili oil atop the dish. I like the spice but not the slick, so I've reduced the amount of chili oil to minimize the greasiness.

■ Drain the liquid from the tofu. Cut the tofu into cubes about 1 inch by ½ inch. It doesn't have to be exact.

■ In a small pot over medium heat, put the tofu, 2 cups of the water, and the salt. Bring to a simmer and then turn off the heat. Let the tofu sit in the hot water over the residual heat of the stove while you finish preparing the other ingredients.

■ In a small bowl, combine the remaining 3 tablespoons water and the cornstarch, and stir to combine. Set aside.

■ Preheat a wok over high heat until wisps of smoke rise from the surface. Add the vegetable oil, onions, ginger, and garlic, and stir-fry quickly for 10 to 15 seconds. Add the ground pork and chili bean sauce, and stir-fry well to combine.

■ Gently add the tofu and the steeping water. Very gently stir the sauce and tofu to combine, and then simmer for 2 to 3 minutes. Add additional salt to taste. Gradually stir in the cornstarch slurry to thicken the sauce. If it looks like it's getting too thick, don't use all of the slurry. Add the peppercorns and give it one last gentle stir. Drizzle on the sesame oil. To serve, drizzle the chili oil on top of the tofu. Serve with steamed rice.

NOTE: I use Pixian chili bean sauce imported from the Sichuan Province (see page 25), which you have to purchase from a Chinese grocery store. You can use your favorite Chinese chili sauce or a combination of chili sauces.

宮保雞

Kung Pao Chicken

MAKES 4 SERVINGS

For the sauce:

2 tablespoons water

1 tablespoon plus 1½ teaspoons soy sauce

1 tablespoon bean sauce, plus more as needed

1 tablespoon minced fresh ginger

1 tablespoon Shaoxing wine or dry Marsala wine

2 teaspoons chili sauce

1 teaspoon sugar

2 large cloves garlic, crushed

½ teaspoon freshly ground Sichuan peppercorns (optional)

1 pound chicken thighs, cut into ¾-inch cubes (about 2 cups)

1 tablespoon soy sauce

1 tablespoon cornstarch

3 tablespoons vegetable oil, divided

1 cup diced sweet bell peppers (about 1-inch dice)

2 stalks green onions, finely chopped

¼ cup Huang Fei Hong Hot Chilli Pepper Peanuts, or roasted unsalted peanuts

Kosher salt

Suggested pairings: Mongolian Beef (page 229) or Simple Stir-Fried Greens (page 137).

This is one of those dishes that I didn't eat often as a child because I didn't like peanuts or bell peppers. The restaurant version we served back then also included water chestnuts, which, to this day, I don't enjoy. But I rediscovered kung pao chicken a few years ago when a student requested a recipe. My palate has grown to crave the spicy, salty, slightly sweet flavors, and I now appreciate peanuts and bell peppers. My secret weapon is a handful of Huang Fei Hong Hot Chilli Pepper Peanuts, which are peanuts seasoned with dried red chilies and Sichuan peppercorns. If you can't find them at your nearest Asian market, you can order them online.

- To make the sauce, in a small bowl, combine the water, soy sauce, bean sauce, ginger, wine, chili sauce, sugar, garlic, and peppercorns. Set aside.

- In a medium bowl, put the chicken and soy sauce, and stir to combine. Add the cornstarch and mix well.

- Preheat a wok over high heat until wisps of smoke rise from the surface. Add 2 tablespoons of the oil and heat until it starts to shimmer. Add the chicken and, using a spatula, spread it into a single layer in the wok. Sear the chicken for 10 to 15 seconds, then stir-fry for 1 minute, or until the chicken is nearly cooked through. Remove the wok from the heat, transfer the chicken to a small bowl, and set aside. Rinse the wok and dry with a towel.

- Return the wok to the stove over high heat. Add the remaining 1 tablespoon oil and heat until it starts to shimmer. Add the bell peppers, and stir for about 1 minute, or until the peppers begin to soften. Add the onions, peanuts, and chicken, and stir for a few seconds to combine. Add the sauce, and stir-fry thoroughly to distribute. Stir-fry for 1 to 2 minutes, or until the chicken is fully cooked through and the sauce has had a chance to meld with the other ingredients. Add a dash of salt or an additional teaspoon bean sauce, to taste, then stir-fry for a few seconds to combine. Serve with steamed rice.

三杯雞

Three-Cup Chicken

MAKES 4 SERVINGS

- 1½ pounds chicken wing portions (see note)
- 2 stalks green onions, cut into 3-inch segments
- ½ cup plus 1 teaspoon vegetable oil, divided
- 4 slices fresh ginger, cut on the bias (about 2 inches long and ⅛ inch thick)
- 4 large cloves garlic, gently smashed
- 3 tablespoons sesame oil
- 3 tablespoons soy sauce
- 3 tablespoons Shaoxing wine or dry Marsala wine
- 1 tablespoon rock sugar or brown sugar
- 1 cup loosely packed fresh basil, very roughly chopped

Suggested pairings: Simple Stir-Fried Greens (page 137) or Stir-Fried Shoestring Potatoes (page 142).

I love the savory, finger-licking quality of this dish. This recipe serves four only if you are serving a couple of other dishes too. The Chinese name of this dish, *san bei ji*, refers to the equal ratio of the three key ingredients: soy sauce, rice wine, and sesame oil. *Bei* is a generic term for "cup" or "glass," but it's often misinterpreted to mean an eight-ounce US measuring cup. It's always made with bone-in chicken, which has more flavor. This dish requires frying. I tried broiling the wings as an alternative, but the texture just isn't the same.

■ Using a cleaver, cut the wing portions in half across the bones. To do this, place the heel of the cleaver blade at the midpoint of one wing. Make sure to grasp the knife firmly at the point the handle meets the blade to get the most stability. Raise the cleaver and bring it down forcefully in one chop to cut through the bones. Repeat with the remaining wings.

■ Place the flat side of your knife on the onion whites and, using the heel of your opposite palm, press or gently pound the knife to smash the onion.

■ Preheat a wok over high heat until wisps of smoke rise from the surface. Add ½ cup of the vegetable oil and heat for about 30 seconds, or until it starts to shimmer. Alternatively, use a deep fryer. In two batches, fry the wing pieces for 3 to 4 minutes, or until the edges of the skin have picked up some golden to caramel color. Gently turn the pieces on occasion to make sure they fry evenly. Strain the wings and set aside. Repeat with the remaining wings. Carefully pour out the oil into a heatproof container to let it cool before disposing. Rinse the wok and dry with a towel.

■ Return the wok to the stove over high heat. Add the remaining 1 teaspoon vegetable oil, the green onions, ginger, and garlic, and stir-fry for about 10 seconds to release the aromas. Add the chicken and stir-fry for a few seconds to combine. Add the sesame oil, soy sauce, wine, and sugar, and stir-fry to combine well. The sauce will bubble vigorously. Continue to stir and toss for 1 to 2 minutes, or until the chicken and the sauce look well integrated. Reduce the heat to medium and simmer for about 2 minutes more, or until the sauce has reduced to about 2 tablespoons and looks like a glaze. Add the basil, and toss again. Serve with steamed rice.

NOTE: You can use a combination of drummettes and wing portions, or just drummettes. If you don't have the ability to cut the wings in half, you can leave the pieces whole. If whole, add an extra 1 to 2 minutes of cooking time at each stage.

雪豆雞片（絲）

Chicken with Snow Peas

MAKES 4 SERVINGS

For the sauce:

2 tablespoons water

1 tablespoon soy sauce

¼ teaspoon sesame oil

2 large cloves garlic, crushed

¾ pound boneless, skinless chicken thighs

1 tablespoon soy sauce

1 teaspoon cornstarch

1 tablespoon vegetable oil

12 to 15 snow peas, trimmed

Suggested pairings: Beef with Pickled Chinese Mustard Greens (page 156) or Spicy Clams with Chinese Sausage (page 165).

This recipe is so flexible that it works with beef, pork, shrimp, and even scallops. If you are using beef or pork, be sure to slice the meat one-eighth inch thick by about three inches long. Use peeled and deveined shrimp and medium scallops. If sugar snap peas are in season, you can use them instead of snow peas. For a splash of color, add julienned carrots.

- To make the sauce, in a small bowl, put the water, soy sauce, sesame oil, and garlic, and stir to combine. Set aside.

- Cut the chicken thighs into roughly ¾-inch cubes. In a medium bowl, put the chicken and soy sauce, and mix well. Add the cornstarch and mix well again.

- Preheat a wok over high heat until wisps of smoke rise from the surface. Add the vegetable oil and heat until it starts to shimmer. Add the chicken and, using a spatula, spread it into a single layer in the bowl of the wok. Sear for about 15 seconds, and stir-fry for 1 to 2 minutes more, or until the chicken is nearly cooked through.

- Add the peas and stir-fry for 1 minute, or until they turn dark green. Add the sauce and stir-fry for 1 to 2 minutes more, or until any larger pieces of chicken are cooked through. Serve with steamed rice.

冬菇蘆筍炒牛肉

Beef with Asparagus

and Shiitake Mushrooms

MAKES 4 SERVINGS

For the sauce:

1 tablespoon soy sauce

1 tablespoon water

1 teaspoon minced fresh ginger

1 teaspoon Shaoxing wine or dry Marsala wine

1 to 2 large cloves garlic, crushed

½ pound flank steak

1 tablespoon soy sauce

1 teaspoon cornstarch

2 tablespoons vegetable oil, divided

½ pound fresh asparagus, trimmed and cut into 1½-inch segments

6 to 8 medium dried shiitake mushrooms, soaked in warm water to reconstitute, stems removed, caps sliced in half

¼ teaspoon sesame oil

¼ teaspoon white pepper powder

Suggested pairings: Kung Pao Chicken (page 151) or Stir-Fried Shoestring Potatoes (page 142).

I remember my mother making this dish specially for my father, because he liked asparagus. But I didn't understand the allure of asparagus until I was an adult and had moved to Seattle, where I experienced the springtime frenzy surrounding the local harvest: asparagus paired with salmon, lamb, morels, and so on. Now, when spring rolls around, I make this dish. While I prefer beef in this stir-fry, you just as easily could cook it with chicken or pork, or go meatless.

- To make the sauce, in a small bowl, put the soy sauce, water, ginger, wine, and garlic, and stir to combine. Set aside.

- Trim the flank steak of any large pieces of membrane. Cut the flank in half or thirds lengthwise, or with the grain. Depending on the total width of the flank, you may get two or three sections that are about 3 inches wide. Cut these sections against the grain into ⅛-inch slices. Place the beef in a medium bowl. Add the soy sauce and mix well. Add the cornstarch and mix well again.

- Preheat a wok over high heat until wisps of smoke rise from the surface. Add 1 tablespoon of the vegetable oil and heat until it starts to shimmer. Gently add the beef and, using a spatula, quickly spread it into a single layer in the bowl of the wok. Sear the beef for about 15 seconds and then stir-fry for 1 to 2 minutes, breaking up any pieces that have stuck together. Remove the wok from the heat, transfer the beef to a medium bowl, and set aside. Rinse the wok and dry with a towel.

- Return the wok to the stove over high heat. Add the remaining 1 tablespoon vegetable oil and heat until it starts to shimmer. Add the asparagus and mushrooms and stir-fry for 1 to 2 minutes, or until the spears have turned dark green. Add the beef and stir to combine. Add the sauce, and stir-fry for 1 to 2 minutes, or until the sauce has penetrated all the ingredients. Add the sesame oil and pepper, and give it one last stir. Serve with steamed rice.

酸菜炒牛肉

Beef with Pickled Chinese Mustard Greens

MAKES 4 SERVINGS

½ pound flank steak

1 tablespoon plus 1 teaspoon soy sauce, divided

1 teaspoon cornstarch

1 tablespoon plus 1 teaspoon vegetable oil, divided

1 chili pepper, such as jalapeño or serrano, sliced

1 cup thinly sliced Pickled Chinese Mustard Greens (recipe follows) or store-bought

2 tablespoons water

1 tablespoon Shaoxing wine or dry Marsala wine

¼ teaspoon white pepper powder

Suggested pairings: Baby Bok Choy with Chicken (page 135) or Dry-Fried Green Beans (page 147).

This classic combination of beef with pickled Chinese mustard greens appears in stir-fries, soups, noodles, and even dumplings. And yet it's a flavor revelation to many Western palates. Many years ago, I made this dish for a party, and one friend fell so in love with it that she insisted on coming to my apartment soon after to learn how to cook it. She even brought the flank steak.

■ Trim the flank steak of any large pieces of membrane. Cut the flank in half or thirds lengthwise, or with the grain. Depending on the total width of the flank, you may get two or three sections that are about 3 inches wide. Cut these sections against the grain into ⅛-inch slices. Place the sliced beef in a medium bowl. Add 1 tablespoon of the soy sauce, and mix well. Add the cornstarch and mix well again.

■ Preheat a wok over high heat until wisps of smoke rise from the surface. Add 1 tablespoon of the oil and heat until it starts to shimmer. Gently add the beef and, using a spatula, spread it into a single layer in the bowl of the wok. Let the beef sear for about 15 seconds and then stir-fry the beef for 1 to 2 minutes more, breaking up any pieces that have stuck together. Remove the wok from the heat, transfer the beef to a medium bowl, and set aside. Rinse the wok and dry with a towel.

■ Return the wok to the stove over high heat. Add the remaining 1 teaspoon oil and heat until it starts to shimmer. Add the chili pepper, and fry for a few seconds to combine. Add the mustard greens, and stir-fry a few seconds to combine. Add the beef, the remaining 1 teaspoon soy sauce, the water, and the wine, and stir-fry for 1 to 2 minutes, or until the sauce has thickened slight. Add the white pepper powder and stir to combine. Serve with steamed rice.

Pickled Chinese Mustard Greens

MAKES ABOUT 1 PINT

¾ pound Chinese mustard greens (about 1 to 2 heads)

1 tablespoon kosher salt

For the brine:

1 teaspoon kosher salt, divided

1 cup room-temperature water

Pickled Chinese mustard greens (*gai choy*) are widely available at Asian markets, but they usually include preservatives and food coloring to make the greens seem more vibrant in the clear packaging. The coloring doesn't affect the flavor, but, if you plan ahead, you can ferment your own greens. You'll need a sterilized pint canning jar.

■ Trim the outer leaves of the greens of any wilted edges. Slice the head of greens in half lengthwise through the core. Cut out the core and reserve. Thoroughly wash the leaves and core, and shake off the excess water. The outer leaves can be unruly and wide. If needed, cut larger leaves in half or thirds lengthwise. Slice the leaves crosswise in strips about ⅛ inch thick, and place in a large bowl. Add the salt. Make sure your hands are very clean and work the salt by hand thoroughly into the sliced greens. Let the greens sit for 20 to 30 minutes.

■ In the meantime, to make the brine, in a small bowl, place the salt and the water, and stir to dissolve. Set aside.

■ Using your hands, work the greens again, massaging and squeezing out the juices. The idea is to create some of the brine in which the greens will ferment. Place the greens into a pint canning jar and push down, packing the greens as tightly as you can. Pour the juices into the jar. Using your fingers, push down some more to squeeze out any air pockets and to generate more liquid. Lodge the core in the jar so that the sliced greens are fully submerged (this is necessary). If needed, add some of the prepared brine to fill the jar, leaving a ¾-inch headspace. Cap the jar so that the lid is firm but not so tight that the gases from the fermentation process can't escape. Set the jar out of direct sunlight in a spot in your kitchen that has a consistent temperature. Let the greens ferment for 7 to 10 days. Store the jar in the refrigerator until you're done eating the greens.

陳皮牛

Orange Beef

MAKES 4 SERVINGS

For the sauce:

⅓ cup orange juice

2 tablespoons plus 1½ teaspoons soy sauce

2 tablespoons water

1 tablespoon Shaoxing wine or dry Marsala wine

For the marinade:

1 tablespoon orange juice

1 tablespoon soy sauce

1 teaspoon Shaoxing wine or dry Marsala wine

2 medium cloves garlic, crushed

¾ pound flank steak

1 large tangerine

3 tablespoons cornstarch

¾ cup plus 1 teaspoon vegetable oil, divided

2 to 3 dried red chili peppers, cut in half crosswise

1 stalk green onion, cut into 3-inch segments

1½ teaspoons sugar

1 teaspoon freshly ground Sichuan peppercorns

Chopped fresh cilantro (optional)

This dish is popular in Chinese restaurants, where it's often batter fried and drenched in a goopy sauce. Traditionally, the dish is made with dried orange peel (*chen pi*) that you buy in Chinese herb shops. Among its purposes, dried orange peel is used to help settle the stomach. I often use fresh orange peel instead, which results in a brighter hint of citrus flavor. For Chinese New Year, oranges—because of their golden color—are auspicious and therefore incorporated into the celebration feast.

▪ To make the sauce, in a small bowl, put the orange juice, soy sauce, water, and wine, and stir to combine. Set aside.

▪ To make the marinade, in a medium bowl, put the orange juice, soy sauce, wine, and garlic, and stir to combine.

▪ Trim the flank steak of any large pieces of membrane. Cut the flank in half or thirds lengthwise, or with the grain. Depending on the total width of the flank, you may get two or three sections that are about 2½ to 3 inches wide. Cut these sections against the grain into ¼-inch slices. Add to the sliced beef to the marinade and set aside to marinate for 10 minutes.

▪ Using a peeler or sharp paring knife, gently peel strips of zest from the tangerine. Avoid the white pith, which is bitter. You want about five to six pieces that are roughly 2 inches long and about ½ inch wide. The pieces don't have to be exact. Set aside.

▪ To the beef, add the cornstarch, and mix well to coat all the pieces so that the beef will develop a thin crust when it cooks. Set aside.

▪ Line a dinner plate with a few layers of paper towels. Set aside.

▪ Preheat a wok over high heat until wisps of smoke rise from the surface. Add ¾ cup of the oil and heat for 1 minute, or until it starts to shimmer. In two to three batches, place the beef in the oil and fry for about 30 seconds on each side, or until the beef is caramelized and crispy on the edges . The oil will sputter, so be careful. Stir-fry the beef for 1 minute more until the beef is nearly cooked through. Transfer the beef to the prepared paper towel–lined plate. Work quickly and repeat with the remaining beef. You may have to decrease

→

the heat if the oil seems to be overheating. Once you're done searing the beef, clean out the wok. Pour the frying oil into a heatproof container to cool, and then discard.

▪ Return the wok to the stove over high heat and heat until wisps of smoke rise from the surface. Add the remaining 1 teaspoon oil and heat until it starts to shimmer. Add the tangerine zest, chili peppers, and onions, and stir-fry for about 30 seconds to release the aromas. Add the sauce and the sugar. It will sputter a bit. Let it heat through for about 10 seconds. Add the beef and stir for a few seconds to coat. Continue to stir-fry the beef in the sauce for 1 to 2 minutes to allow it to heat through and finish cooking. Sprinkle with the peppercorns and mix well again. Garnish with the cilantro and serve.

香乾肉絲

Five-Spice Tofu Gan

with Slivered Pork and Celery

MAKES 4 SERVINGS

- 8 to 10 ounces pork loin chop, cut into slivers
- 1 teaspoon soy sauce
- 1 teaspoon Shaoxing wine or dry Marsala wine
- 1 teaspoon cornstarch
- 2 tablespoons plus 1½ teaspoons vegetable oil, divided
- 8 ounces of five-spice *tofu gan*, sliced (see page 36)
- 1 to 2 stalks green onions, cut into 3-inch segments
- 1 small jalapeño, thinly sliced (optional)
- 2 medium stalks celery hearts, sliced ⅛ inch thick on the bias
- ½ medium carrot, finely julienned
- 1 tablespoon plus 1½ teaspoons soy sauce

Suggested pairings: Dry-Fried Green Beans (page 147) or Wok-Seared Corn and Green Onions (page 138).

This is one of those dishes that tastes of home. My brothers request it when I host a big family dinner. If we all go out to a Chinese restaurant, we always order *xian gan rou si*. The key is to make sure the tofu and the meat are seared. I like using celery hearts because they're more tender. We often have to double this recipe so that there are leftovers. You can use beef or chicken, if you prefer.

■ In a small bowl, put the pork, soy sauce, and wine, and mix well. Add the cornstarch and mix well again.

■ Preheat a wok over high heat until wisps of smoke rise from the surface. Add 1 tablespoon of the oil and heat until it starts to shimmer. Add the pork and, using a spatula, spread it in the wok. Sear for about 15 seconds and then stir-fry for about 15 seconds more, or until nearly cooked through. Remove the pan from the heat, transfer the pork to a small bowl, and set aside. Rinse the wok and dry with a towel.

■ Return the wok to the stove over high heat. Add the remaining 1 tablespoon plus 1½ teaspoons oil and heat until it starts to shimmer. Add the tofu; using a spatula, spread it into a single layer in the bowl of the wok, and sear for 30 seconds, or until the edges are browned. Flip the tofu and sear for 30 seconds more. This is not an exact science. If some pieces aren't seared, it's okay. Quickly and gently push the tofu up the sides of the wok. Add the onions and jalapeño, and stir-fry for about 10 seconds to combine. Add the celery and carrots, and stir-fry with the tofu for a few seconds to distribute.

■ Add the pork and soy sauce, and stir-fry for about 2 minutes, or until the sauce has penetrated the tofu. Serve with steamed rice.

回鍋肉

Twice-Cooked Pork

MAKES 4 SERVINGS

- 2 teaspoons vegetable oil
- ½ medium red or yellow bell pepper, cut into thin strips
- 1 small jalapeño, sliced
- 2 stalks green onions, cut into 2-inch segments
- 2 large cloves garlic, smashed
- ½ to 1 cup braising liquid from Red-Braised Pork Belly (page 187) (see note)
- 1 teaspoon finely minced ginger
- 2 cups sliced Red-Braised Pork Belly (page 187) and about

Suggested pairings: Simple Stir-Fried Greens (page 137) or Vegetarian's Delight (page 226).

"You make this better than I do," my mother said to me. At the restaurant, she would throw a small chunk of pork shoulder into the deep fryer for a couple of minutes to parcook. Then she would slice the pork and stir-fry it with green bell peppers, green cabbage, onions, and chili sauce. For our family, however, she would make twice-cooked pork only when there was leftover red-braised pork shoulder. We'd all hover over the plate, wishing there was more. Now, because twice-cooked pork traditionally uses pork belly, I use leftovers from making Red-Braised Pork Belly (page 187). I always cook a little extra pork belly so that I can whip up this dish the next day.

■ Preheat a wok over high heat until wisps of smoke rise from the surface. Add the oil and heat until it starts to shimmer. Add the bell peppers and stir-fry for about 30 seconds, or until they start to soften. Add the jalapeño, onions, and garlic, and stir-fry for a few seconds to combine. Add the braising liquid and the ginger, and stir-fry for a few seconds before adding the pork belly. Stir-fry for 1 to 2 minutes to heat through. As the pork comes back to temperature and the sauce coats all the ingredients, everything will start to look glossy, and the sauce will reduce and thicken. Serve with steamed rice.

NOTE: Be sure to strain the braising liquid before using. If the liquid has been in the refrigerator, it will be solid. You can add the gelled braising liquid directly to the stir-fry.

辣味蛤蠣炒香腸

Spicy Clams

with Chinese Sausage

MAKES 4 SERVINGS

2 links Chinese sausage, sliced on the bias into ¼-inch-thick pieces

½ cup finely julienned fresh ginger

2 stalks green onions, finely chopped

1 small jalapeño, cut into ¼-inch-thick slices

1½ pounds manila clams, cleaned

¼ cup Shaoxing wine or dry Marsala wine

1 tablespoon soy sauce

Suggested pairings: Simple Stir-Fried Greens (page 137) and Chicken with Snow Peas (page 153).

Clams in black bean sauce is so ubiquitously appreciated that the combination has even appeared on the menu at one of my favorite non-Asian restaurants in Seattle. But I didn't grow up eating a lot of dishes that used these fermented black beans, which is an ingredient more common to the Cantonese cooking of southern China. My parents favored the flavors that span from Sichuan to Shanghai to Taiwan and points farther north. When I think of stir-frying clams, I think of ginger, green onions, and fresh green chilies. For this recipe, I include Chinese sausage for a hint of sweetness to temper the spice.

■ Preheat a large soup pot or Dutch oven over medium-high heat for about 15 seconds and add the sausage. Cook for about 1 minute, or until the fat starts rendering and the edges are browned. Flip the sausage and cook for 1 minute more.

■ Add the ginger, onions, and jalapeño, and stir to combine. Add the clams, wine, and soy sauce, and stir to distribute. Reduce the heat to medium. Steam, covered, 7 to 8 minutes, or until the clams open. Serve.

湯品、燉燒類

Soups and Braises

There is life force in a big pot of soup. A memory, a curative, a gift of love, or a promise of a full belly infuses each soup or braise that I make. Every once in a while, my mother reminds me how much I loved chicken soup as a toddler. I've heard the anecdote so many times, it has become a memory. In fifth grade, when we were able to visit Taipei for the first time after we'd immigrated to the States, I recall going to this little restaurant that specialized in soups. I lifted the lid on my bowl, which revealed a black chicken foot and the most delicately rich, gingery broth I had ever tasted. Once I graduated college and got my first newspaper job ten hours by car from home, my visits to my family always began with a hug from my mother and a bowl of her chicken soup. When my father was ailing, I made him ***mian pian tang***, a soup with large noodle squares. He was a stoic man, but hunched over a bowl of soup, he could forget his ill health for a moment and offer a rare compliment. The first days after my daughter was born, my mother made me chicken soup and winter melon soup to help me heal and to encourage my body to produce more milk for my infant.

What I most love about these soups is that they are either quick and simple, or, if they take a little more effort, they yield multiple meals. Sometimes, the best soups aren't even formal recipes. They arise from leftovers and, like an improvised fiddle tune, are deliciously fleeting. There have been plenty of occasions when I've added water and soy sauce to leftover stir-fry to create a soup to eat with rice, or "remixed" leftover soup to give it new life. It's good to have a free spirit in the kitchen sometimes.

Much like a long-simmering broth, braising gives time for meats to relax and become tender. "Red-braising" is the term that the Chinese use to describe anything braised in soy sauce, which gives dishes a mahogany color. Filling the house with the aromas of red braises always wins me points with the family. They know that something wonderful is on the way. Similar to soups, a second-meal incarnation of a red-braised dish can be even better than the original. The Red-Braised Pork Belly, for example, is already a star dish. But leftover pork belly recast as Twice-Cooked Pork will make your eyes roll back into your head. It's definitely worth tending the pot for an afternoon.

番茄蛋花湯

Tomato Egg Drop Soup

with Ginger

MAKES 4 SERVINGS

- 2 tablespoons vegetable oil
- 1 cup diced fresh tomatoes (see note)
- 2 stalks green onions, chopped
- ¼ cup soy sauce
- 2 to 3 teaspoons grated fresh ginger
- 5 cups water
- 2 packed cups fresh baby spinach
- 3 large eggs
- ½ teaspoon sesame oil
- Chopped fresh cilantro (optional)

The egg drop soup most commonly served in Chinese restaurants is pale, thickened with cornstarch, and bland. We served that style of egg drop soup for twenty-three years at my family's restaurant. But when we made egg drop soup for ourselves, we made this version. Sometimes, my mom would add a handful of fresh spinach at the end. I've taken the liberty of adding fresh ginger to punch up the flavor; you can adjust the amount of ginger according to your preference.

▪ Preheat a small soup pot over high heat for about 10 seconds. Add the vegetable oil and heat until it starts to shimmer. Add the tomatoes, onions, soy sauce, and ginger, and stir for about 30 seconds to soften the tomatoes. Add the water and bring the soup to a slow boil, then reduce the heat to medium low. Add the spinach and stir.

▪ Beat the eggs in a small bowl. To drizzle the eggs into the soup, slowly pour the eggs through the tines of a whisk or fork as you move in a circular motion around the pot. This helps to create "ribbons" of egg. The egg will float to the surface; stir to break it up a bit.

▪ Drizzle the soup with the sesame oil, garnish with the cilantro, and serve immediately as a starter.

NOTE: There's no need to seed or peel the tomatoes. You can use your choice of tomatoes, especially when they're in season and extra juicy.

酸辣湯

Hot-and-Sour Soup

MAKES 4 TO 6 SERVINGS

3 ounces pork, slivered (see note)

⅓ cup soy sauce plus 1 teaspoon soy sauce, divided, plus more as needed

1 teaspoon vegetable oil

6½ cups water, divided

¼ cup white vinegar, plus more as needed

2 teaspoons freshly ground white pepper, plus more as needed

1 small block medium or firm tofu, cut into strips

¼ cup dried tree ear fungus, soaked in warm water to reconstitute, and sliced

1 cup bamboo shoot strips

6 dried shiitake mushrooms, soaked in warm water to reconstitute, sliced

½ cup cornstarch

3 large eggs, beaten

1 teaspoon sesame oil

Chopped green onions, for garnish (optional)

Chopped fresh cilantro, for garnish (optional)

Suggested pairings: Red-Braised Pork Belly Pot Stickers (page 103) or Green Onion Pancakes (page 90).

I have made more hot-and-sour soup than I can quantify. By the time I started college, I was responsible for cooking three daily soups at my family's restaurant: egg drop, chicken corn, and hot-and-sour. We had a deep thirty-six-inch wok that could accommodate more than eighty servings. Traditional hot-and-sour soup is considered a curative and contains ingredients such as dried tiger lily buds, tree ear fungus, pork, and sometimes blood tofu (blood pudding). We made a simplified version for our Midwestern customers that included tofu, bamboo shoot strips, canned button mushrooms, and eggs. When we made the soup for ourselves, we would include a small amount of pork and plenty of shiitake mushrooms. The other key flavor is the white pepper powder, which gives the soup a more nuanced spice.

- In a small bowl, put the pork and 1 teaspoon of the soy sauce, and mix well.

- In a large soup pot over high heat, heat the oil until it starts to shimmer. Add the pork and, using a spatula, stir-fry for 1 minute, breaking up any pieces that have stuck together. Add 6 cups of the water, the remaining ⅓ cup soy sauce, the vinegar, and pepper, and stir to combine. Add the tofu, tree ear fungus, bamboo shoots, and mushrooms. Let the mixture come to a boil, then reduce the heat to medium or medium low so that the soup is at a gentle bubble.

- In a small bowl, combine the cornstarch and the remaining ½ cup water. In consecutive slow pours, add the cornstarch slurry to the soup while stirring with a cooking spoon. The soup will start to thicken. When the soup returns to a simmer, drizzle the egg on top. I like to pour the beaten egg in a steady, circular stream so that it creates "threads." The hot liquid will cook the egg immediately. When the egg blossoms, give the soup a gentle stir to incorporate the egg. Add more soy sauce, vinegar, and pepper to taste. Drizzle the soup with the sesame oil, garnish with the onions and cilantro, and serve.

NOTE: I like to buy boneless pork loin chops. They're usually ½ to ¾ inch thick and sold two to a pack. The soup doesn't require much meat. Or, if I have a piece of pork shoulder in the house, I'll cut off a small piece to freeze and use when needed. I cut the pork into fine strips to match the bamboo shoots and tofu.

雞湯

Chicken Broth

MAKES ABOUT 3 TO 4 QUARTS

- About 3 to 4 pounds bone-in chicken parts or 1 whole chicken
- About 4 quarts water, plus more as needed
- ¼ cup soy sauce
- ¼ cup Shaoxing wine or dry Marsala wine
- 2 stalks green onions, cut into 3-inch segments
- 3 slices fresh ginger, cut on the bias (about 3 inches long and ¼ inch thick)
- 8 small or medium dried shiitake mushrooms, soaked in warm water to reconstitute
- 2 teaspoons kosher salt, plus more as needed

Since I was old enough to eat it, I have loved this chicken broth ladled over rice with shiitake mushrooms. My mom would make this soup with a whole chicken, and that's how I've made it for most of my adult life. The broth simmers until the chicken is fork tender and perfect for dipping in soy sauce—something my brothers and I would do as children. Now, I sometimes make a more pungent dip for the chicken that includes soy sauce, sesame oil, chili sauce, minced cilantro leaves and stems, green onions, and garlic. When I want to make the chicken stretch, however, I carve out the breast pieces to set aside for stir-frying. The broth still gets enough flavor from the rest of the meat and carcass, and the breast meat usually yields enough protein for an oversize portion of stir-fry. While this soup is great on its own, it's also the base for Wonton Soup (page 178), Simple Hot Pot (page 181), and Chinese Cabbage and Tofu Soup (page 177). Its soothing properties come from the combination of the meaty, rich notes and the hint of warm spice from the ginger.

■ In a large stockpot over high heat, bring the chicken and water to a boil, skimming off the scum as it floats to the surface. Reduce the heat to low. Add the soy sauce, wine, onions, ginger, and mushrooms, and give it one stir to combine. Let simmer for 2 to 3 hours, or until the broth has developed good, rich flavor. Check the broth from time to time, continuing to skim the top layer for scum or rendered fat. After about 1 hour of simmering, taste the broth. It should have a light chicken flavor. Add 2 teaspoons salt, and gently stir. Let the broth continue to simmer for 1 to 2 hours more. Along the way, if the broth has bubbled along too eagerly and lost some volume, add 1 to 2 cups of water.

■ If you are serving the broth immediately, add additional salt to taste to balance the flavor. Ladle the soup into bowls with pieces of chicken and shiitake mushrooms.

■ If you are using this broth as a base for a soup, you can strain the broth for a smoother consistency. The broth will keep in the refrigerator for about 3 days or in the freezer for several months.

蟹肉玉米濃湯

Corn and Dungeness Crab Soup

MAKES 4 SERVINGS AS A STARTER OR 2 SERVINGS AS A MAIN

2 tablespoons cornstarch

2 tablespoons water

6 cups Chicken Broth (page 173) or water, or 2 cups broth plus 4 cups water

2 cups fresh or frozen corn kernels

2 cups lump Dungeness crabmeat or other crab of choice

2 tablespoons Shaoxing wine or dry Marsala wine

1 tablespoon rice vinegar

1 to 2 teaspoons kosher salt, plus more as needed

1 teaspoon finely minced fresh ginger

¼ teaspoon freshly ground white pepper

2 cups roughly chopped Chinese broccoli or other leafy greens such as kale or spinach

2 large eggs, beaten

½ teaspoon sesame oil

On the West Coast, we are fortunate enough to enjoy the meaty Dungeness crab. In season, we locals who have access to crab pots and a boat head out to set traps. When luck is on our side, we catch our quota within a few hours. I like to save some crab meat to make corn soup. If you don't have access to Dungeness, you can use your favorite type of crab. This preparation also works well with minced chicken.

- In a small bowl, combine the cornstarch and water, and stir to combine. Set aside.

- In a 3-quart pot, combine the broth, corn, crabmeat, wine, vinegar, salt, ginger, and pepper. Bring to a boil over high heat, then reduce the heat to low and simmer for 10 minutes. Add the greens and continue to simmer for 2 minutes more. Add the cornstarch slurry and stir well to combine. Swirl in the egg in as fine a stream as you can, so you get threads of egg and minimize the clumping. Add the sesame oil, and stir once, adding more salt to taste. Serve steaming hot.

麵疙瘩湯

Dumpling Knots Soup

(Mian Ge Da Tang)

MAKES 4 SERVINGS

2 cups all-purpose flour

About ¾ cup water

1 small bundle bean thread noodles, soaked in warm water to reconstitute

1 tablespoon vegetable oil

3 ounces minced chicken thigh or breast, or ground chicken

2 quarts Chicken Broth (page 173)

3 cups thinly sliced Chinese cabbage

4 medium dried shiitake mushrooms, reconstituted and sliced

Kosher salt

2 large eggs, beaten

½ teaspoon sesame oil

This thick soup is what I crave when I have a cold, or if there's ever leftover chicken broth. The dumpling knots (*mian ge da*) are pillows of comfort. The beauty of this soup is that it actually can be made with any number of ingredients. If I don't have enough broth, I add water. The meat is optional, and bok choy or other leafy greens work just as well as the Chinese cabbage.

■ Put the flour in a medium bowl. Swirl half of the water into the flour. Using chopsticks or a fork, mix so that small, shaggy pieces of dough (dumpling knots) start to form. Swirl in the remaining water and continue to stir to create more shaggy pieces of dough. The point is to create shards of dough of different sizes and shapes. If you end up with some larger pieces that are bigger than gnocchi, you can break them up. If there is still loose flour in the bowl, sprinkle 1 or 2 tablespoons more water on it and stir. Set aside.

■ Drain the bean thread. Give the bundle two or three cuts crosswise with scissors so that they're easier to eat. Set aside.

■ Heat a wok over high heat until wisps of smoke rise from the surface. Add the oil and heat until it starts to shimmer. Add the chicken and stir-fry for about 1 minute, until browned. Add the broth, cabbage, and mushrooms, and bring to a boil. Lower the heat to medium. Add the noodles and cook for 1 to 2 minutes. In batches, carefully add the dumpling knots, stirring as you go to keep them from sinking to the bottom of the pot. Adjust the heat as needed and simmer the soup for 2 to 3 minutes more, or until the largest pieces of dumpling have cooked through. Drizzle in the egg and stir a few times to distribute. Add the sesame oil and stir. Serve steaming hot.

白菜豆腐湯

Chinese Cabbage and Tofu Soup

MAKES 4 SERVINGS

- 2½ quarts Chicken Broth (page 173)
- 3 cups sliced Chinese cabbage (2-inch squares)
- 1 (14-ounce) package soft or medium tofu, cut into ¾-inch cubes
- 1 small bundle bean thread noodles, soaked in warm water to reconstitute
- Kosher salt

Chinese cabbage and tofu is a classic combination that speaks to the essence of a Chinese person. They pair so well in any number of stir-fries, soups, or braises. This soup is a no-brainer: if there's a good broth—or even if there isn't—you add cabbage and tofu, some bean thread, and, alongside a bowl of rice, you have a meal.

■ In a medium Dutch oven or soup pot over high heat, bring the broth to a boil. Add the cabbage and tofu and let the soup return to a boil, then reduce the heat to medium low and simmer for about 15 minutes, or until the cabbage has softened. Add the bean thread and simmer for 2 to 3 minutes more. Add salt to taste. Serve with steamed rice.

餛飩湯

Wonton Soup

MAKES 4 TO 6 SERVINGS

40 to 45 Wontons (page 97)

3 quarts Chicken Broth (page 173)

½ pound baby bok choy, trimmed and leaves separated

½ teaspoon sesame oil

Chili sauce, for serving

The wonton soup I grew up on was not the wonton soup my parents served in our restaurant. Because it sold for a dollar fifty a bowl, that version literally paled in comparison to the soup we made at home. Where the restaurant soup had to be fast and cheap, our home-style soup featured a slowly developed, rich broth and more voluptuous wontons. Maybe customers would've paid more if they had known just how delicious wonton soup could be.

■ Boil the wontons according to the recipe. Meanwhile, in a 7- to 8-quart pot, bring the broth to a boil over high heat, and then reduce the heat to low. Add the bok choy to the broth to blanch while the wontons finish cooking.

■ Using a spider or large slotted spoon, transfer the cooked wontons to the broth. Let simmer for 1 to 2 minutes, or until the bok choy are tender. Drizzle the sesame oil over the soup, and stir. Serve with chili sauce on the side.

火鍋

Simple Hot Pot

Hot pot is the Asian version of fondue. People gather around a burbling pot of broth, dipping an assortment of thinly sliced meats, vegetables, seafood, noodles, and any number of other ingredients into it. There aren't firm rules to hot pot, because you can serve it with any flavor of broth and any combination of proteins and vegetables, in individual hot pots or using a communal pot. Either way, it's a sumptuous meal that brings people together. I have many memories of sitting with my parents and brothers around a burbling pot of broth filled with goodies. An electric wok is not really useful for stir-frying, but we had one for hot pot. We kids learned early on how to handle steaming-hot Chinese cabbage, bean thread noodles, fish balls, and soup. I think that, because I was brought up on soups like this, I've never found cold soups appealing.

In Mandarin, hot pot is called *huo guo*, which literally translates to "fire pot." Regional influences and personal preference dictate whether the broth is mild, made with medicinal herbs, or loaded with fiery chilies and hot oil. At hot pot restaurants, you get a menu with a list of ingredients, and you check the items you want. Some restaurants have tables with an inset induction burner. Others provide a tabletop butane burner topped with a pot of broth. If you get a yin-yang pot, which has a divider in the center, you get two types of broth. Once the broth is simmering, you add all the Chinese cabbage, which is the core ingredient and tastes best after it has softened. Other quick-cooking ingredients, such as the thinly sliced meats, are heated in the broth briefly and then dipped into your choice of condiments, ladled into your rice bowl, and then eaten with a bite of rice. Some contemporary hot pot restaurants, such as the Boiling Point chain, offer personal hot pots that arrive on special stands equipped with Sterno "canned heat." You're just as likely to see individual diners enjoying a hot pot at such a restaurant as a group of boisterous friends. It's wonderful.

If you go to a Chinese market, you will easily find all the materials for hot pot. Stores set up displays with stacks of tabletop butane burners that sell for less than twenty dollars. Be sure to grab a pack of fuel, which is usually situated nearby. The pots tend to be aluminum, and they are also inexpensive. They are typically sold with a glass lid. Alternatively, you can buy an electric hot pot or a tabletop induction burner and an appropriate pot. All of these items are easily available online through Amazon, though it'll likely cost less if you go to an Asian market.

→

Equipment:

When searching for equipment online, look for "hot pot" or *shabu-shabu*, which is the Japanese term for hot pot.

- 1 single-burner butane stove or tabletop electric or induction burner. Alternatively, you can buy a dedicated electric hot pot. These are widely available online, in Asian markets, or at restaurant supply stores.
- 1 Asian-style hot pot or a Dutch oven (at least 3½ quarts). You can find hot pots at Asian markets or online. If you get a yin-yang pot, it will have a divider in the middle that allows you to serve two kinds of broth.
- 1 hot pot strainer per person. These are wire strainer scoops that help you fish out any meat or vegetables that you have added to the broth.
- 1 rice bowl or other small soup bowl per person.
- 1 side plate or sauce dish per person.
- 1 soupspoon, preferably a Chinese-style ceramic soupspoon, per person.

Ingredients:

---

3 TO 4 QUARTS BROTH: Hot pot restaurants offer a variety of broths that range from plain to incendiary, and some even have proprietary blends of seasonings. At home, I use Chicken Broth (page 173) for the base. If you want to make the broth spicy, you can add 12 or more dried red chili peppers, 3 tablespoons Chili Oil (page 99), 1 teaspoon Sichuan peppercorns, 1 teaspoon white pepper powder, 1 star anise, 1 tablespoon *sa cha* (see page 25), and kosher salt to taste.

The amounts of the following ingredients vary according to how much you can eat. Start with 2 heaping cups of cabbage per person and ¼ to ½ pound of assorted meats and seafood per person. Add other ingredients according to your preference.

VEGETABLES: The one ingredient that every hot pot contains is Chinese cabbage. The rest is up to personal preference. Some options: any variety of leafy Asian and other greens (bok choy, spinach, pea shoots, watercress, green leaf lettuce), thinly sliced winter melon, thinly sliced potato or squash, mushrooms (shiitake, enoki, wood ear, oyster), lotus root, bamboo shoots, and so on.

MEATS: Asian markets sell meats sliced paper thin specifically for hot pot. Butchers partially freeze the cuts of meat and then run them through the meat slicer. The variety of cuts of beef, pork, lamb, and chicken include shoulder, loin, belly, leg, breast, and offal. If you don't have access to an Asian market, buy the cuts of meat you'd like and freeze them for several hours, just long enough to help you slice paper-thin pieces. If you have great technique and a very sharp knife, you can do this without freezing the meat.

MEATBALLS: Asian markets sell many types of frozen meatballs made of beef, pork, cuttlefish, white fish, roe-filled fish, or shrimp. Japanese-style fish cakes are also a great addition.

SEAFOOD: Any kind of fish that you may find in a stew would work well. Shrimp, squid, scallops, clams, and mussels are also good options.

OTHER INGREDIENTS: Soft-cooked quail eggs, different types of tofu, wontons, wheat noodles, bean thread noodles, and dumplings.

DIPPING SAUCES: Chili sauce, chili bean sauce, hoisin sauce, Soy-Ginger Dipping Sauce (page 72), Black Vinegar with Chili-Garlic Sauce (page 109), Ginger-Scallion Oil (page 104), or Fermented Bean Curd Sauce (recipe follows).

Fermented Bean Curd Sauce

MAKES ABOUT ¼ CUP

- 1 teaspoon fermented bean curd in chili
- 3 tablespoons vegetable oil
- 2 tablespoons hoisin sauce
- 1 teaspoon honey

Use this sauce for dipping cooked hot pot ingredients. Fermented bean curd is available in jars at Asian markets. It's pungent and salty, so you need only a little bit at a time. It's handy to keep a jar in the refrigerator for making sauces or marinades, or to eat with congee.

▪ Put the bean curd in a small bowl, and gently mash it. Add the oil, hoisin, and honey, and whisk together until smooth. You can store the sauce in an airtight container in the refrigerator indefinitely. The oil will separate, so give it a quick stir before using.

火腿冬瓜湯

Winter Melon Soup

with Smoked Ham Hock

MAKES 4 TO 6 SERVINGS

- 2½ quarts water
- 1 small smoked ham hock or shank (see note)
- 2 slices fresh ginger, cut on the bias (about 2 inches long and ⅛ inch thick)
- 1 stalk green onion
- 2 tablespoons soy sauce
- 2 tablespoons Shaoxing wine or dry Marsala wine
- 1 (2-pound) wedge winter melon, cut into 2-inch chunks

My husband has proclaimed winter melon soup his favorite. It has a clear broth made from smoked ham hock, ginger, green onions, a splash of soy sauce for color, and wine. The winter melon goes in at the end and offers a counterpoint to the smokiness. You don't want to cook the winter melon too long or it starts to lose its shape and "melt" into the soup. I usually serve this soup at Chinese New Year or deep in the Northwest winter when it feels like it can't get any darker or damper. This recipe does require a trip to an Asian grocery store for the winter melon, which is a type of gourd that looks like a misshapen watermelon when whole. Few home cooks ever need a whole winter melon, so stores often sell precut wedges.

▪ In a large Dutch oven or soup pot over high heat, put the water, ham, ginger, onions, soy sauce, and wine, and stir to combine. Bring the broth to a gentle boil, then reduce the heat to low and simmer for 1 to 1½ hours, or until the flavor of the ham has come through.

▪ After about 1 hour of simmering the broth, taste for seasoning. If it tastes too salty, remove the hock and add a little bit of water to balance it out.

▪ Add the winter melon and simmer for 15 to 20 minutes, or until the melon becomes tender but before it disintegrates. You can serve the soup with bits of the smoked hock meat picked off the bone.

NOTE: The size of the smoked hock or shank and how it was smoked will affect the flavor. Some will be saltier than others, but you may not know until you've started cooking the soup.

排骨海帶湯

Pork Spare Ribs

and Kelp Soup

MAKES 4 SERVINGS

- 8 cups water
- 1 pound pork riblets or loin back ribs, cut between the bones into individual pieces
- 3 slices fresh ginger, cut on the bias (about 2 inches long and ⅛ inch thick)
- 1 stalk green onion, cut into three segments
- 1 tablespoon soy sauce
- 2 teaspoons kosher salt, plus more as needed
- 15 (2-inch) squares kelp (see note)
- 1 to 1½ cup soybean sprouts

Based on a very small sample—my husband and children—the flavor combination in this soup may be an acquired taste. I love it, though. My mother would make this soup occasionally when I was growing up, and I have two clear memories associated with it: First, I particularly liked eating the kelp and would fish out as many pieces as I could. Second, I dreaded the task of plucking the unruly roots off the soybean sprouts, even if I enjoyed eating them. I realize now that trimming the roots is not necessary; it was just my father's preference. The ginger and the kelp have anti-inflammatory properties too.

■ Combine the water and pork ribs in a large soup pot over high heat. Bring to a boil, then reduce the heat to low. Skim off any foamy scum, and continue to skim as the broth develops. Add the ginger and onions, and simmer for about 40 minutes. Add the soy sauce, salt, kelp, and sprouts. Continue to simmer for 20 more minutes. Taste for seasoning. If you think it needs a touch more salt, add it to taste. Ladle the soup into four bowls with a bit of the sprouts, kelp, and a rib for each person.

NOTE: Kelp comes in different sizes. It can be large sheets or 2-inch squares. If you get a sheet, you will have to soak the sheet in warm water for 15 minutes before cutting it into smaller pieces.

紅燒肉

Red-Braised Pork Belly

MAKES 4 SERVINGS

1 pound skin-on pork belly

7½ cups water, divided

¼ cup Shaoxing wine or dry Marsala wine

3 tablespoons soy sauce

1 tablespoon plus 1½ teaspoons rock sugar

2 stalks green onions, cut into 3-inch segments

3 to 4 large slices fresh ginger, cut on the bias (about 3 inches long and ¼ inch thick)

3 to 4 cloves garlic, gently smashed

1 star anise

Suggested pairings: Simple Stir-Fried Greens (page 137) or Dry-Fried Green Beans (page 147).

This recipe keeps changing, and yet it stays the same. My mother used to use skin-on pork picnic shoulder roast for red-braised pork (*hong shao rou*), because it was more widely available and relatively inexpensive. She would make the braise soupier in order to generate extra sauce for rice and add a little cornstarch slurry to thicken the sauce. I switched to using pork belly because I like getting the perfect bite of skin, fat, and meat, a three-layer texture and flavor bomb.

At Asian markets, small slabs of raw, skin-on pork belly are commonly available. You can get prepackaged pieces that are about one pound in weight or have the butcher cut pieces to order. If you don't have access to an Asian market, you will have to visit a butcher shop or make a special order from your preferred market. It's essential to have the belly with skin on or it won't hold its shape during cooking. If you prefer to have leaner meat, use pork shoulder in your braise. There is still enough marbling that the meat will taste good; it just won't have the silkiness of the belly.

I like to serve this dish on a bed of stir-fried baby bok choy leaves. I look for smaller heads of baby bok choy, so that I can separate the leaves and cook them whole. Asian markets tend to stock baby bok choy in different sizes, so you can choose according to your needs. If all you can find are the large half-pound heads, then cut up the leaves according to the Simple Stir-Fried Greens recipe (page 137).

This is the pork belly that is featured in Red-Braised Pork Belly Pot Stickers (page 103). If you plan on the traditional *gua bao* sandwich (see page 105), you should cut the belly into ½-inch-thick by 2½-inch-long slices instead of squares. This will make the pork belly easier to slip into the folded bun with all the condiments.

▪ Position the pork belly with the skin side down. Using a sharp knife, cut the pork belly into roughly 1½-inch-square pieces. The skin will take a little extra pressure to cut through, so be careful. Combine the pork and 3 cups of the water in a 4- or 5-quart pot. Bring to a boil over high heat, then reduce the heat to low. Simmer for 5 minutes to release some of the scum. Turn off the heat and, using a slotted spoon or tongs, transfer the pork to a medium bowl. Discard the water and carefully rinse out the pot.

▪ Return the pot to the stove over high heat. Add the pork belly, 4 cups of the water, the wine, soy sauce, sugar, onions, ginger, garlic, and star anise, bring

→

the mixture to a boil, and then reduce the heat to low. Simmer for about 1 hour, checking occasionally and stirring to make sure all the meat pieces spend some time submerged in the braising liquid. After an hour, if the sauce seems overly salty, add the remaining ½ cup water. Check the tenderness of the largest piece of pork belly with a fork. If there's any resistance, the pork will need to simmer for 10 to 15 minutes more. As the pork simmers, the sauce will continue to reduce, intensify in flavor, and become a caramel. After 10 minutes, repeat the fork test. Once the pork belly is tender, increase the heat to medium to speed up the reduction process. Stir constantly to prevent sticking and to ensure that all the pork belly pieces are evenly coated with the caramel. When nearly all of the liquid has reduced, remove the pot from the heat. Arrange the pork belly on a serving plate or bowl, and serve with steamed rice.

LU ROU VARIATION

In Taiwan, braised meat sauce with rice (*lu rou fan*) is a universally loved bowl-food dish. It's made in a similar fashion to Red-Braised Pork Belly but has three main departures: the meat is cut into smaller pieces, fried shallots are added, and you stew hard-boiled eggs in the braising liquid to accompany the dish. Follow the instructions in the Red-Braised Pork Belly recipe, but cut the pork belly into ½-inch pieces. When adding the soy sauce, wine, and other aromatics, add 1 cup of Fried Shallots (recipe follows) or use store-bought, ¼ teaspoon freshly ground Sichuan peppercorns, 3 cloves, and 6 peeled hard-boiled eggs. Braise for 30 to 40 minutes, or until the pork is tender.

Be sure to turn the eggs on occasion to make sure all sides benefit from stewing in the liquid. Slice the eggs in half. Serve the pork over rice, with the stewed eggs.

Fried Shallots

While you can buy fried shallots at an Asian market, the packages are usually quite large and can become rancid if you don't use them up quickly. Frying your own is easy enough to do.

MAKES ABOUT 1 CUP

6 to 8 medium shallots
2 cups vegetable oil

■ Line a dinner plate with several layers of paper towels.

■ Trim and peel the shallots. Slice the shallots crosswise about ⅛ inch thick.

■ Heat the oil in a small skillet over medium heat until the oil starts to shimmer. Add the shallots, in batches if needed, and fry for 3 to 4 minutes, or until golden brown. Using a slotted spoon or a spider, transfer the shallots to the paper towel–lined plate; they will continue to brown slightly and also crisp up. Use right away, or store in a covered container in the pantry for up to 3 days.

滷牛腱

Sliced Red-Braised Beef Shank

MAKES 4 TO 6 SERVINGS

- 1½ to 2 pounds boneless beef shank (see note)
- 12 cups water, divided
- ½ cup plus 1 tablespoon soy sauce, divided
- ½ cup dry white or red wine (whatever you have on hand)
- 1 tablespoon rock sugar or light brown sugar
- ½ teaspoon whole Sichuan peppercorns
- 3 large slices fresh ginger, cut on the bias (about 3 inches long and ¼ inch thick)
- 2 stalks green onions, cut into three segments
- 4 to 6 large cloves garlic, lightly smashed
- 2 dried red chili peppers
- 1 star anise
- ½ teaspoon sesame oil, for serving
- Chopped fresh cilantro, for garnish

Chilled sliced beef shank, drizzled with soy sauce and sesame oil, is a common snack, appetizer, or sandwich filling. I have distinct memories of using slices of shank, especially the pieces with extra marbling, to sop up soy sauce and sesame oil in order to maximize each perfect bite. For sandwiches, my father would stuff beef slices between a folded piece of toasted white bread. He also loved packing this sliced beef—and soy sauce eggs and, sometimes, braised duck wings—for our family road trips. The beef needs to chill overnight, so plan accordingly. The extra braising liquid in this recipe can be strained, skimmed of fat, and served over rice.

▪ Cut the shank into 4 large pieces. In a 4- or 5-quart pot, combine the shank and 6 cups of the water. Bring to a boil over high heat. As the water comes to temperature, the beef will constrict and the top edges will pop above the water. That is okay at this stage. Reduce the heat to medium low and simmer for about 5 minutes. Remove the pan from the heat and transfer the beef to a medium bowl. Discard the water and rinse the pot.

▪ Return the pot to the stove. Combine the beef with the remaining 6 cups water, ½ cup of the soy sauce, the wine, sugar, peppercorns, ginger, onions, garlic, chili peppers, and star anise. Bring to a boil over high heat, then reduce the heat to low. Simmer for 1½ to 2 hours, or until the beef is tender to the bite. Remove the pot from the heat and transfer the beef to a large covered container. (Strain the braising liquid and reserve to serve with rice, if you'd like.) Chill overnight.

▪ To serve, slice the beef very thinly and drizzle it with the remaining 1 tablespoon soy sauce and the oil. Garnish with cilantro.

NOTE: Asian markets are your best bet for finding boneless beef shank. If you don't have easy access to an Asian market, you can use bone-in beef shank. Typically, bone-in shanks are sliced like thick steaks. You can braise them bone-in and remove the bone once the meat is tender.

燒餅夾滷牛肉

Red-Braised Beef Shank

with Shao Bing Sandwiches

MAKES 8 SANDWICHES

8 pieces Sesame Flatbread (Shao Bing) (page 95) or store-bought

About 24 slices Sliced Red-Braised Beef Shank (page 189)

2 tablespoons soy sauce

1 teaspoon sesame oil

1 cup Pickled Chinese Mustard Greens (page 157) or store-bought, finely chopped

Cilantro sprigs, for garnish

Chili sauce (optional)

There isn't really a sandwich culture in Chinese cooking. Filled buns are more prevalent. *Shao bing*, or sesame flatbread, is an exception. It can be eaten on its own, but it's often used as a wrap. In this case, it's like a pita sandwich. You don't have to make your own *shao bing*, but they are worth the extra step. You can also purchase frozen *shao bing* and toast them. When you make a batch of the Sliced Red-Braised Beef Shank, there is always plenty of extra beef to fill these sandwiches.

▪ If the *shao bing* are not fresh from the oven, warm them in the oven at 350 degrees F for about 5 minutes. Carefully slice open the bread, keeping one seam intact.

▪ Arrange the beef slices on a plate. Drizzle the soy sauce over the beef. Then drizzle the oil over the beef. Be sure every piece comes in contact with the soy sauce.

▪ Place about 3 slices of the beef in each *shao bing*. Top the beef with one-eighth of the mustard greens and sprigs of cilantro. Add the chili sauce. Serve.

糖醋排骨

Sweet-and-Sour Spare Ribs

MAKES 4 SERVINGS

- 2 pounds "sweet-and-sour" cut pork spare ribs
- 7 cups water, divided
- ½ cup soy sauce
- ¼ cup Chinese black vinegar or balsamic vinegar
- ¼ cup rock sugar or brown sugar
- ¼ cup Shaoxing wine or dry Marsala wine
- 4 to 6 large cloves garlic, smashed
- 3 stalks green onions, cut into 3-inch segments

Suggested pairings: Simple Stir-Fried Greens (page 137) or Dry-Fried Green Beans (page 147).

Sweet, sour, salty, meaty. Done. It really doesn't get any easier to pull together a dish that has such a great payoff. Asian markets often keep the "sweet-and-sour" cut of pork spare ribs in stock. If your local store doesn't have it, you can ask the butcher to cut a rack of ribs for you. If you prefer beef, kalbi-style short ribs would work with this recipe too, but you'll have to check for tenderness much sooner since kalbi ribs are sliced so thinly.

■ Cut the ribs into individual riblets. To do this, look at the back of the rack of ribs, where it should be easier to see the bones. Make cuts between the bones to create riblets.

■ In a large Dutch oven over high heat, put the ribs and about 3½ cups of the water, making sure the ribs are covered. Bring to a boil, then reduce the heat to medium low. Simmer for about 5 minutes to release some of the scum. Remove the pan from the heat and transfer the ribs to a large bowl. Rinse the pot.

■ Return the pot to the stove. Add the ribs, the remaining 3½ cups water, the soy sauce, vinegar, sugar, wine, garlic, and onions. Bring to a boil over high heat, then reduce the heat to low and simmer, stirring occasionally, for 45 minutes. Check the largest piece of rib for tenderness. If it's fork tender, increase the heat to medium high and let the sauce reduce, stirring occasionally, for about 15 minutes. As the sauce reduces, the sugars will caramelize and the sauce will get thicker and stickier. Watch and listen very carefully to the pot. When the sauce has reduced enough that you can hear sizzling and see the bottom of the pan, remove the pan from the heat. Serve as an appetizer or with rice as part of a meal.

紅燒獅子頭

Lion's Head Meatballs

MAKES 4 TO 6 SERVINGS

1 pound ground pork (see note)

2 tablespoons soy sauce

1 tablespoon Shaoxing wine or dry Marsala wine

1 teaspoon finely minced fresh ginger

1 teaspoon sesame oil

1 stalk green onion, finely chopped

1 cup vegetable oil

½ pound Chinese cabbage

1 quart water

1 teaspoon kosher salt, plus more as needed

1 small bundle bean thread noodles, soaked in warm water to reconstitute

Suggested pairings: Ginger-Onion Whole Steamed Fish (page 202) or Simple Stir-Fried Greens (page 137).

I so love humble dishes that give more than they take. This is such a dish. It's soupy and hearty without being heavy. I make the meatballs with ground Kurobuta pork and shape them about the size of a tennis ball. The meatballs in this dish are usually double the size—hence the name "lion's head." The dimpled Chinese cabbage leaves cook down around the meatballs and look like the lion's mane. I love how the cabbage and the cellophane noodles absorb the savoriness. It's so good, I've actually stood at the stove eating the cabbage straight out of the pot.

▪ In a large bowl, place the ground pork, soy sauce, wine, ginger, sesame oil, and onions, and mix very well. Divide the meat mixture into 6 portions and shape each into a meatball.

▪ Preheat a wok over high heat until wisps of smoke rise from the surface. Add the vegetable oil and heat until it begins to shimmer. Using a slotted spoon, gently lower 3 meatballs into the oil. Brown the meatballs for 2 to 3 minutes on each side, adjusting the heat as needed. You don't need to cook the meatballs all the way through. Transfer the meatballs to a dinner plate. Repeat with the remaining meatballs.

▪ Cut the core out of the Chinese cabbage. Leave the inner leaves whole. Cut the larger, outer leaves into segments. It's okay if the pieces are large, because by the time the braise is done, the cabbage leaves will have cooked down. If the pieces are too small, they'll "melt."

▪ In a Dutch oven large enough to hold all the meatballs, add the cabbage leaves and place the browned meatballs on top of the cabbage. Add the water and bring to a boil over high heat. Reduce the heat to low. Simmer for about 45 minutes, uncovered, or until the broth tastes delicious and the cabbage has cooked down.

▪ Stir in the salt, adding additional to taste, if necessary. Submerge the noodles in the broth and let them soften for about 5 minutes. Serve with rice as a part of a meal.

NOTE: I like to use ground Kurobuta pork or a similar heirloom-breed pork. The flavor is cleaner and the marbling makes it juicier. If you don't have access to this specialty pork, I recommend using *unseasoned* sausage mix, which includes a touch of fat. Ground pork you typically find packaged in grocery stores is too lean and will yield a dry meatball.

辣豆豉燒鱸魚

Chili Black Bean Cod

MAKES 4 SERVINGS

- ¾ cup plus 2 tablespoons water, divided
- 2 tablespoons cornstarch
- 2 teaspoons vegetable oil
- 3 stalks green onions, finely chopped
- 2 tablespoons finely minced ginger
- 4 to 5 large cloves garlic, crushed
- ½ cup Shaoxing wine or dry Marsala wine
- 2 tablespoons chili black bean sauce
- 1 heaping tablespoon fermented bean curd in chili (optional)
- 1 tablespoon Chinese black vinegar or balsamic vinegar
- 1 pound black cod fillets
- ½ teaspoon sesame oil

Suggested pairing: Simple Stir-Fried Greens (page 137). Use a hearty green, such as Chinese broccoli (*gai lan*) or yu choy.

The Chinese love whole fish for the value and, during Chinese New Year, its symbolism of good fortune. The masters—like my mother—know how to pick the bones clean for all the flavorful bits. That said, it's not always convenient to cook a whole fish. That's when fillets come to the rescue. Black cod is a meaty fish that can take on this pungent sauce.

■ In a small bowl, add 2 tablespoons of the water and the cornstarch, and stir to combine. Set aside.

■ Preheat a wok over high heat until wisps of smoke rise from the surface. Add the vegetable oil, immediately followed by the onions, ginger, and garlic. Stir-fry the aromatics for about 30 seconds, or until the onions are fragrant. Add the remaining ¾ cup water, the wine, bean sauce, bean curd, and vinegar. Stir to break up the bean curd and combine the sauce. Once the sauce comes to a simmer, add the cod fillets. Reduce the heat to low and let the fish simmer in the sauce for 3 to 4 minutes, or until the fish becomes more opaque. Flip the fish to cook on the other side for another 3 to 4 minutes. Increase the heat to medium high. Add the cornstarch slurry to the sauce around the fish. Carefully stir the sauce to incorporate the slurry, shifting the fish fillets as needed. Scoop some of the sauce over the fish as you go. Once the sauce has thickened, about 30 seconds, add the sesame oil. Serve with rice as part of a meal.

喜慶宴會餐點

Celebration

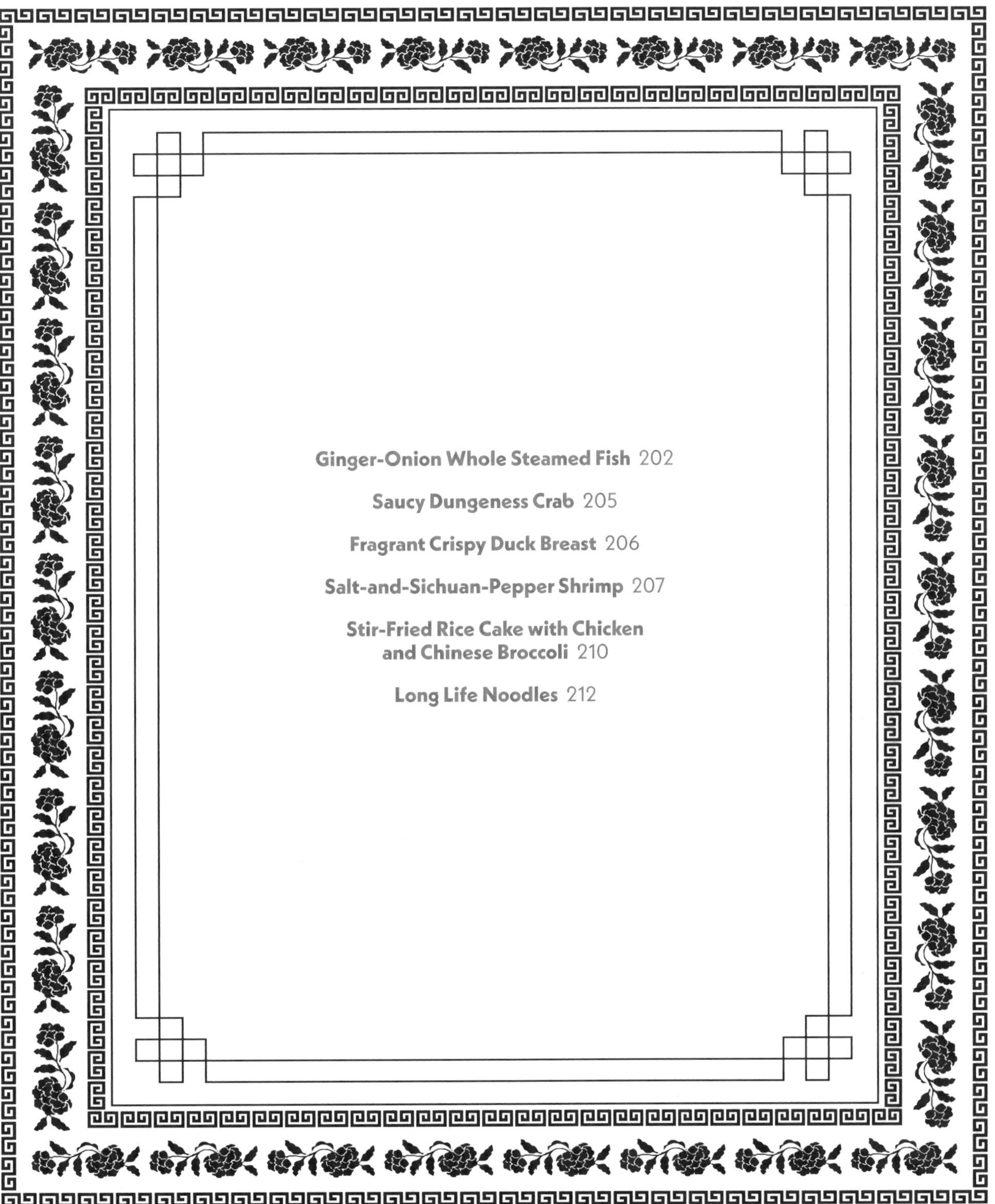

Celebrating Chinese New Year is what centers me. In so many ways, the contours of what used to separate my Chinese upbringing and American influences have become less distinct and more amorphous. I often catch myself skipping the formality and deference that my father would have insisted on. So preparing for the customs and feasting related to Chinese New Year snaps into focus what it means to me to be Chinese. Since my brothers and I all have mixed families, it's this holiday that gives us the opportunity to bridge the valley between our culture and the one that my children and their cousins inhabit.

After my father died, my mother moved in with us. Because she is our matriarch, my home is now the gathering place for our annual reunion feast. Chinese New Year is so ingrained in our lives that everything from how our dining room is arranged to the size of our dinner table is determined, in part, by how they facilitate hosting family for New Year's. The kids get excited because they know they'll be receiving red envelopes filled with money to wish them longevity. I plan, shop, and prep for the meal over several days. The refrigerator starts to groan from being stuffed with ingredients. My commercial-size steamer comes out of the basement storage. Pots and pans that normally sit in the back of the cabinet are enlisted into service.

I have to design the menu to reflect foods that have auspicious qualities conferred upon them by virtue of their shape or symbolic names. Whole fish, with head and tail intact, represents family unity. They also represent prosperity, because one of the phrases you say to wish others good luck and good fortune includes a word that is a homophone for "fish." Tangerines are significant because the color and shape are reminiscent of the gold ingots that used to be used for money, so you will see bowls of tangerines as decoration and as an offering to the ancestors. Extra-long noodles are served to wish people longevity.

I have hosted Chinese New Year as a single young professional, a newlywed, a new mom, and now as the eldest sibling who bears some responsibility to carry on family traditions and mark the milestones of our growing extended family. My mother has seven grandchildren, from an infant to a fourteen-year-old. For her to be able to preside over her legacy is a privilege. Chinese New Year ultimately is about reuniting the family around the table, honoring the elders and the departed, and celebrating our collective good fortune to be in this world.

Chinese New Year Symbols and Superstitions

Chinese New Year, also known as "Lunar New Year" or "Spring Festival," lands according to the lunar calendar, so the actual date varies from year to year. It takes place sometime between January 20 and February 20. Traditionally, the holiday is celebrated over fifteen days. Businesses tend to go on holiday. Students get extended time off too. Family members are expected to return home from wherever they may be in the world. The Chinese calendar also follows a twelve-year cycle, and each year is represented by an animal. Each of the animals in the Chinese zodiac possesses character traits. It's believed that your zodiac sign influences your personality and horoscope. Matchmakers use the zodiac to ensure matches are ideal.

There are so many symbolic foods and superstitions that I learn something new every year. Eight, for example, is a lucky number, so you may see dishes that include eight ingredients or menus that include eight dishes. The pronunciation of eight, "ba," is similar to the word "fa," which is related to wealth and prosperity. Here are some common beliefs and practices around the menu and traditions.

Family Unity, Fertility, Abundance

- Seeds and candies
- Whole fish or poultry
- Lion's head meatballs
- Rice
- Hot pot

Longevity

- Long life noodles
- Rice cake

Good Luck, Wealth, Prosperity

- Tangerines
- Pomelos
- Oysters
- Spring rolls
- Stir-fried rice cake
- Whole fish

Chinese New Year Customs

- Clean the house to get rid of any bad luck. After the New Year, you can't sweep the floor during the first few days or you'll sweep away the good luck.
- Families pay their respects to the elders by kneeling before them and bowing their heads to the floor (kowtowing).
- The elders give children red envelopes filled with money to ensure longevity.
- Everyone wears new clothes.
- People set off firecrackers to scare away evil and bad fortune. They also hang "double-happiness" signs and good-fortune signs.
- Because eight is a lucky number, you will see eight represented in different ways. In the United States, you can order "lucky money" from the Treasury department, which are dollar bills printed with a serial number that starts with four eights. The bills arrive sheathed in plastic and set in a large red card and matching envelope.
- Families that are scattered in different cities all return home for the holiday.
- The feast not only helps to celebrate the holiday, but also creates leftovers.
- You aren't supposed to use a knife in the first few days or it's believed you're cutting off good fortune.

SAMPLE CHINESE NEW YEAR MENU

Cold Plates

- Sliced Red-Braised Beef Shank (page 189)
- Salt-and-Sichuan-Pepper Shrimp (can be served room temperature) (page 207)

Dumplings

- Boiled Pork and Cabbage Dumplings (page 71)

Main Dishes

- Lion's Head Meatballs (page 194)
- Spicy Clams with Chinese Sausage (page 165)
- Ginger-Onion Whole Steamed Fish (page 202)
- Fragrant Crispy Duck Breast (page 206)
- Saucy Dungeness Crab (page 205)
- Stir-Fried Rice Cake with Chicken and Chinese Broccoli (page 210)
- Simple Stir-Fried Greens (page 137) (with baby bok choy)

Soup

- Winter Melon Soup with Smoked Ham Hock (page 184)

Sweets

- Oranges and New Year's candies

蔥薑蒸全魚

Ginger-Onion Whole Steamed Fish

MAKES 4 SERVINGS

1 whole fish, such as striped bass, snapper, or rockfish (about 1½ pounds), scaled and cleaned (ask the fishmonger to do this)

1 to 2 teaspoons kosher salt

6 stalks green onions, cut into 3-inch segments, divided

½ cup finely julienned fresh ginger, divided

3 tablespoons soy sauce

2 tablespoons Shaoxing wine or dry Marsala wine

2 tablespoons vegetable oil

Roughly chopped fresh cilantro, for garnish (optional)

Suggested pairings: Simple Stir-Fried Greens (page 137) or Baby Bok Choy with Chicken (page 135).

This is a classic preparation for a steamed whole fish. The ginger and green onions not only flavor the fish, but also help to temper any fishiness. Serving whole fish during Chinese New Year symbolizes the wish for prosperity throughout the year and many happy returns. When you serve whole fish, remember these serving tips: Point the head toward the most distinguished guest. When one side of the fish has been picked clean of flesh, do not turn the fish, which symbolizes flipping a boat or ship. Simply lift the tail and the carcass will separate itself from the bottom half of the fish.

- Set up your steamer (see page 47) over high heat.

- Score the fish, gently making three to four cuts along the body of the fish on both sides, starting from the dorsal fin to the belly. The cuts should be deep enough that you can stuff them with some ginger and onions. Sprinkle the salt in the slits on both sides to help flavor the fish. Gently place half of the onions and ¼ cup of the ginger into the slits.

- In a small pot over medium-high heat, combine the soy sauce, wine, oil, and the remaining onions and ¼ cup ginger. Heat to a boil and then reduce the heat to low. Keep the sauce over low heat while the fish steams.

- Place the fish in a steam-proof dish, such as a pie plate, that fits in your steamer. The dish should be deep enough to let the sauce pool at the bottom. Steam the fish for 10 to 15 minutes, depending on the size of the fish. To check for doneness, turn off the heat. Carefully lift the lid of the steamer. Using the tip of a sharp knife, gently probe the flesh at the meatiest part of the fish. If it is opaque and flakes, then the fish is done steaming. If it looks underdone, then close the lid and steam over high heat for up to 5 minutes more.

- Remove the dish from the steamer and drizzle the soy sauce mixture over the fish. Garnish with cilantro. Serve with rice as a part of a meal.

炒螃蟹

Saucy Dungeness Crab

MAKES 4 SERVINGS

- 2 whole, live Dungeness crabs (about 4 pounds)
- 2 teaspoons vegetable oil
- 6 large cloves garlic, smashed
- 3 stalks green onions, cut into 2-inch segments
- ¼ cup thinly sliced coins fresh ginger
- ¼ cup Shaoxing wine or dry Marsala wine
- ¼ cup soy sauce
- ¼ cup water

Living in the middle of Missouri meant that any crab we ate was frozen. Eating Alaskan snow crab was a treat, and we would always stir-fry it in this savory sauce. It wasn't until I moved to Seattle that I learned just how diverse and fresh crab can be. The meaty, sweet Dungeness crab is the local specialty. Going crabbing has provided my family—the kids especially—with many memories and sumptuous meals.

■ Bring a large pot of water to a boil over high heat. Add the crabs and boil for 10 to 12 minutes. (The crabs will not be fully cooked; they will finish cooking in the sauce.) Remove the crabs from the pot and place them in the sink. They will be hot, so wear a pair of rubber gloves. Separate the shells from the body. It may take some force to do so. Under a stream of cool water, remove the gills, and, if desired, the yellow crab butter.

■ Break the crab bodies into halves, then segment the legs in pairs. Set aside.

■ Preheat a wok over high heat until wisps of smoke rise from the surface. Add the oil and heat for about 5 seconds, then add the garlic, onions, and ginger. Stir-fry for a few seconds to release the aroma. Add the wine, soy sauce, and water, and stir to combine. Let the sauce come to simmer, then reduce the heat to medium low and add the crab. Let the crab simmer in the sauce for 5 to 6 minutes, or until the meat in the body is no longer translucent. Be sure to stir and shift the crab legs at the bottom to the top and the ones on the top to the bottom to help ensure even cooking. Serve with plenty of napkins.

香酥鴨

Fragrant Crispy Duck Breast

MAKES 4 SERVINGS

About 1 to 1½ pounds skin-on duck breasts

2 tablespoons Shaoxing wine or dry Marsala wine

3 tablespoons Sichuan Pepper Salt (page 208), divided

¼ cup cornstarch, for dredging

¼ cup flour, for dredging

1 tablespoon soy sauce

Vegetable oil, for frying

Suggested pairings: Simple Stir-Fried Greens (page 137) or Dry-Fried Green Beans (page 147).

Crispy duck doesn't get its due. It may not have the ceremony of Peking duck or the accessibility of Chinese barbecued duck, but it has depth of flavor from the dry brine and two-step cooking process. A dusting of flour and deep-frying are what give the duck a crispy skin. At New Year's, it's customary to serve whole duck to symbolize the wholeness of family. But it would be challenging for many home cooks to be able to steam and deep-fry a whole duck. So I've adapted the recipe for duck breasts. The duck needs to brine overnight, so plan ahead.

■ Rinse the duck breasts and pat them dry with paper towels. Using a very sharp knife, score the duck skin with a crisscross pattern. Do not cut into the flesh. Drizzle the breasts with wine, then rub 2 teaspoons of the pepper salt into the duck, especially in the crevices of the skin. Place the duck in a ziplock bag or in a bowl covered with plastic wrap. Let it brine overnight in the refrigerator.

■ The next day, set up your steamer (see page 47) over high heat and bring the water to a boil. Place the duck in a dish deep enough to hold the breasts and the fat that will be rendered during steaming, such as a pie plate. Alternatively, check it during the steaming period and remove excess rendered fat with a baster. Place the dish of duck breasts in the steamer, making sure there is at least 1 inch of space surrounding the plate to allow for the steam to reach the duck. Steam for 45 minutes. Remove the dish from the steamer and transfer the duck pieces to a large plate.

■ In a medium bowl, combine the cornstarch and flour. Drizzle the soy sauce on the flesh side of the breasts, then dredge the duck in the flour mixture.

■ Line a plate with a few layers of paper towels. Set aside. In a wok over medium-high heat, add enough oil to accommodate the thickness of the duck breasts. Heat the oil until it registers 350 degrees F on an instant-read thermometer, then carefully add the duck breasts. Fry for 3 to 5 minutes, or until the duck is golden brown and crispy. Transfer the duck to the prepared paper towel–lined plate to drain. Slice the duck into ½-inch-thick pieces. Arrange the duck on a serving plate, and serve with the remaining pepper salt on the side.

鹽酥蝦

Salt-and-Sichuan-Pepper Shrimp

MAKES 4 APPETIZER SERVINGS

- 1¼ cup vegetable oil, divided
- 3 stalks green onions, finely chopped
- 2 teaspoons finely minced fresh ginger
- 4 large cloves garlic, finely minced
- 1 medium shallot, finely minced (about 2 tablespoons)
- 1 Thai bird chili, sliced (optional)
- ¾ pound headless shrimp in the shell, or 1 pound head-on shrimp in the shell
- 2½ teaspoons Sichuan Pepper Salt (recipe follows), divided
- 1 egg white
- 1 teaspoon crushed garlic
- ¼ cup cornstarch, for dredging
- ½ teaspoon white pepper powder, for serving
- ¼ cup finely chopped fresh cilantro, for serving (optional)

There are many variations of this dish, but the idea is to quickly stir-fry head-on shrimp in the shell with a spice mixture. It's such a savory, lip-smacking dish that it forces you to slow down and suck all the flavor out of the shells and shrimp heads. If my father saw this on a menu at a Chinese restaurant, he'd always order it. This fried version crisps the shell enough that you can eat it, if you choose. You can adapt this recipe for whatever size shrimp you prefer. It's great as an appetizer or as a salty snack during happy hour.

■ Line a plate with paper towels.

■ In a small skillet over medium-high heat, heat ¼ cup of the oil. Add the onions, ginger, garlic, shallots, and chili. Fry the aromatics in the oil for 2 to 3 minutes, constantly stirring for even browning. After about 2 minutes, watch carefully. If they start to brown too quickly, remove the pan from the heat. Strain the aromatics and tip them onto the prepared paper towel–lined plate. Set aside.

■ Rinse the shrimp in cool water and drain. If you have head-on shrimp, you can skip to the next step. If you have headless shrimp, using a pair of kitchen scissors, cut the shell and devein the shrimp. Starting at the "neck" of the shrimp, make a cut that's about ⅛ inch in the flesh of the shrimp where the dorsal vein is located. You will be making an incision in the flesh and also cutting the shell, but do not remove the shell. Cut only to the bottom of where the body tapers to the tail. It will look like a stunted effort to butterfly the shrimp. Rinse the vein area under running water and remove. Repeat with the remaining shrimp. Drain any excess water.

■ In a large bowl, put the shrimp, 1 teaspoon of the pepper salt, the egg white, and garlic. Carefully mix with tongs or a spoon to combine. Set aside. In a shallow dish, such as a pie plate, place the cornstarch. Set aside.

■ In a wok over medium heat, heat the remaining 1 cup oil. If necessary, adjust the amount of oil for the size of the pan for shallow frying. Alternatively, you can also use a deep fryer.

→

■ Lightly dredge 3 to 4 shrimp at a time in the starch. Fry the shrimp for about 1 minute per side, or until the shrimp have turned pink and the shells are crispy. Transfer the cooked shrimp to a large bowl. Repeat with the remaining shrimp. Add the fried aromatics, and sprinkle on the white pepper and the remaining 1½ teaspoons pepper salt. Toss thoroughly. Arrange on a platter or in a bowl, and top with the cilantro.

Sichuan Pepper Salt

MAKES ABOUT 3 TABLESPOONS

2 tablespoons whole Sichuan peppercorns

1 teaspoon white pepper powder

1 tablespoon sea salt or kosher salt

In addition to seasoning shrimp, you can use any leftover pepper salt for non-Chinese dishes, including steak or roasted chicken.

■ Pick through the peppercorns and discard any large stems. Don't worry about the smaller stems.

■ In a small, dry skillet over medium-low heat, toast the peppercorns for about 2 minutes, or until fragrant. Gently shake the pan as they toast to make sure you don't burn the peppercorns. Once toasted, tip the peppercorns onto a plate to cool. Grind the peppercorns to a fine powder in a spice grinder. In a small bowl, place the ground Sichuan peppercorns with the white pepper and salt, and mix well. This pepper salt can be stored in an airtight container on the counter for several months.

上海年糕炒芥蘭

Stir-Fried Rice Cake

with Chicken and Chinese Broccoli

MAKES 4 SERVINGS

- 6 ounces chicken breast, cut into 1½-inch-long slivers (about ¾ cup)
- 1 tablespoon plus 1 teaspoon soy sauce, divided
- 1 tablespoon cornstarch
- 2 tablespoons vegetable oil, divided
- 3 cups chopped Chinese broccoli (*gai lan*) leaves, with a few thinly sliced stems mixed in
- 2 cups water
- 2 cups sliced rice cake
- 1 tablespoon hoisin sauce
- 1 tablespoon Shaoxing wine or dry Marsala wine
- ¼ teaspoon freshly ground white pepper
- ½ teaspoon sesame oil

Rice cake is called *nian gao*, or "sticky cake," in Mandarin. It's treated like a pasta and used in soups or stir-fry dishes. Serving rice cake for Chinese New Year is symbolic because the words for "sticky" and "year" are homophones. Serving rice cake represents a wish for many happy new years to come. Look for sliced rice cake in the refrigerated aisle of an Asian market.

▪ In a small bowl, combine the chicken and 1 teaspoon of the soy sauce, and mix well. Add the cornstarch and mix well again.

▪ Preheat a wok over high heat until wisps of smoke rise from the surface. Add 1 tablespoon of the vegetable oil and heat for 5 seconds. Spread the chicken in a thin layer in the wok. Sear the slivers for about 30 seconds, then stir-fry the chicken for about 1 minute until cooked through. Remove the wok from the heat, transfer the chicken to a small bowl, and set aside. Rinse the wok and dry with a towel.

▪ Return the wok to the stove over high heat. Add the remaining 1 tablespoon vegetable oil and heat for 5 seconds. Add the broccoli and stir-fry for about 1 minute. Add the water and the rice cake, and stir to combine. Reduce the heat to medium and let simmer for about 2 minutes, or until the rice cake becomes reconstituted and has softened. Add the hoisin, the remaining 1 tablespoon soy sauce, and the wine, and stir-fry to combine. If it looks soupy, increase the heat to high to reduce the sauce, but keep stir-frying so that the rice cake doesn't stick to the bottom of the wok. Add the pepper and sesame oil, and give it one last stir before removing the wok from the heat. Serve hot.

長壽麵

Long Life Noodles

MAKES 4 SERVINGS

For the sauce:

- 1 cup water
- 2 tablespoons soy sauce
- 1 tablespoon hoisin sauce
- 1 teaspoon minced fresh ginger
- 1 stalk green onion, finely chopped
- 1 large clove garlic, minced

- 2½ cups all-purpose flour, plus more for dusting
- ¾ cup warm tap water
- ½ pound raw shrimp, size 16/20, peeled and deveined
- 1 teaspoon soy sauce
- 2 teaspoons cornstarch
- 1 tablespoon plus 1 teaspoon vegetable oil, divided
- 1 stalk green onion, cut into 2-inch segments
- ½ medium carrot, julienned (about ½ cup)
- 3 to 4 cups roughly chopped greens, such as baby bok choy, yu choy, or Chinese broccoli
- ½ teaspoon sesame oil, for drizzling
- Kosher salt

For New Year's and birthdays, it's customary to wish people a long life by serving this symbolic dish. It's important never to cut the noodles and leave them as long as possible. If you make your own noodles, you can make them even longer than what you might find at the market. If you aren't able to make your own noodles, you can use store-bought dried or fresh noodles instead.

■ To make the sauce, in a small bowl, put the water, soy sauce, hoisin sauce, ginger, onions, and garlic, and mix well. Set aside.

■ Put the flour in a large bowl, and gradually add the water. Using a rubber spatula, wooden spoon, a pair of chopsticks, or your fingers, stir the water and flour together. Continue to stir gently until the dough starts to form into a ball. Now, using your hands, knead the dough and incorporate any remaining flour. Knead the dough a few times to make a ball. The dough should feel slightly tacky but not damp. It should not stick to your fingers.

■ Lightly dust your work surface with flour. Remove the dough from the bowl and knead for about 2 minutes, or until smooth. Cover the dough with plastic wrap and let it rest for at least 20 minutes. (While it doesn't need much longer than that, it won't hurt the dough if it happens to rest longer.)

■ Line a baking sheet with parchment paper. Set aside.

■ Once rested, lightly dust your work surface with flour, and knead the dough by hand for about 2 minutes, or until smooth. Divide the dough into four sections and work with one section at a time. Shape each piece of dough roughly into a rectangle. (If you start with a rectangular shape, you are more likely to roll out a rectangular sheet.)

■ Roll out the first piece of dough, trying your best to maintain the rectangular shape, until it is about ⅛ inch thick. It will be slightly thinner than a store-bought flour tortilla. The rolled-out dough will be about 18 inches long by 7 to 8 inches wide. Dust your work surface and the dough generously with flour as you go.

■ Once you have rolled out the rectangle, trim any stray edges so that you have relatively even sides. Dust the surface with flour. Fold the rectangle of dough in half lengthwise, so that you join short edge to short edge. Dust the dough with flour and fold that in half again. Turn the dough so that the folds are facing you. Using a sharp knife, cut noodles that are about ¼ inch in width. Dust the cut noodles with flour and use your hands to unfurl the strands. Place the noodles in a loose bundle on the prepared baking sheet. Repeat with each of the remaining sections of dough. (To cook the noodles later, see note.)

■ In a large pot over high heat, bring about 4 quarts of water to a boil. Set 1 cup of cold tap water on the counter next to the stove.

■ In a medium bowl, put the shrimp and soy sauce, and mix well. Add the cornstarch and mix well again. Set aside.

■ When the water is boiling, drop the noodles into the pot. Stir immediately to keep the noodles from clumping. The noodles will take about 3 to 5 minutes to cook, so don't walk away. When the water begins to bubble up, add about ½ cup of the cold water to keep the noodles at a manageable simmer. Add additional cold water as needed. Test a noodle. It should be cooked through but still have a tiny bit of chew. Drain and use immediately.

■ If you aren't using the noodles immediately, you can "shock" them under running cold tap water to cool them off and keep them from becoming a giant noodle brick. When ready to serve, dip the noodles in hot, simmering water for about 1 minute to bring them back to temperature.

■ Preheat a wok over high heat until wisps of smoke rise from the surface. Add 1 tablespoon of the vegetable oil and heat for about 5 seconds, or until it starts to shimmer. Add the shrimp and, using a spatula, stir-fry the shrimp for 2 to 3 minutes, or until they turn pink. Remove the wok from the heat, transfer the shrimp to a medium bowl, and set aside. Rinse the wok and dry with a towel.

■ Return the wok to the stove over high heat. Add the remaining 1 teaspoon vegetable oil and the onions, and stir for about 5 seconds to release the aroma. Add the carrots and greens, and stir-fry for about 1 minute to combine. Add the shrimp and the sauce, and stir again to combine. Add the noodles and carefully stir-fry to mix with the other ingredients for about 1 minute, or until the sauce has penetrated the noodles. It may be helpful to use tongs. Once well combined, drizzle the sesame oil over the noodles. Remove the wok from the heat. Add a dash of soy sauce or a pinch of salt to taste, if needed. Serve.

NOTE: After you cut the noodles, you can freeze them to use later. Place the noodles in small bundles on the parchment-lined baking sheet, freeze for about 1 hour, then transfer the bundles to a ziplock bag to finish freezing. When ready to cook, do not defrost. Drop the bundles of frozen noodles into boiling water and cook for 4 to 6 minutes.

解饞小品

Guilty Pleasures

My parents started a Chinese restaurant in 1980 in Columbia, Missouri. He had been a career military liaison officer, and she was a well-known journalist in Taipei. Both had master's degrees. But in Columbia, they were the mom and pop who sold egg rolls, fried rice, cashew chicken, sweet-and-sour pork, and other dishes that didn't resemble any Chinese foods they knew. Despite their lack of experience in building a restaurant business, they forged ahead toward the hallowed American Dream. I was eight when I walked into that restaurant. My brother Sam was six, and David Jr. was just several months old. I didn't leave the restaurant until I had graduated journalism school and gotten my first newspaper job.

Our lives revolved around the restaurant. We were there seven days a week except on Thanksgiving, Christmas, and two weeks in the summer. If we kids weren't in school, we were at the restaurant working. At eight, I made wontons. By the time I was in high school, we had moved the restaurant to a bigger location, and I was front of the house, managing an assortment of responsibilities. I was the queen of packing take-out orders, which sometimes outpaced the number of dine-in customers.

We weren't in the restaurant business to fulfill any culinary aspirations. We did, however, learn a lot about Midwestern tastes and how to adapt our menu to cater to our diners. Crab rangoon and General Tso's chicken may not be Chinese, but such dishes constitute an interpretation of Chinese soul food. I describe the recipes in this chapter as "guilty pleasures" because people know they aren't necessarily authentic, but they love them anyway and will eat them even from mediocre take-out places. Don't worry, I'm not one to judge; I enjoy a good General Tso's chicken on occasion too.

BEST CHINESE RESTAURANT?

The question I get most frequently is "What is the best Chinese restaurant?" I always struggle to answer that question because a majority of Chinese restaurants exist as a means to an end. Immigrant families, like mine, started restaurants to make a living. Once in business, the goal is always to appease the customer, and when most customers demand cheap, familiar foods, that's what they get. So it's hard to pick a best restaurant when the restaurants have no intention of maintaining the standards and consistency that would elevate them to "best restaurant" status. That's not to say that there aren't great Chinese restaurants that serve authentic, high-quality foods. They tend to be located in urban areas that have a high density of Chinese residents: New York, San Francisco, Los Angeles, Vancouver (Canada). The one saving grace for those of us who don't live in one of those metropolises is that some mom-and-pop Americanized Chinese restaurants offer a "secret" menu that's reserved for Asians. The specials may be written in Chinese on the wall or there's a separate printed menu or the chef will take requests. The secret menu often contains more traditional dishes. We didn't have a printed secret menu, but if a Chinese VIP guest came to our restaurant, my mother would cook dishes that had more authentic flavors.

雞炒麵

Chicken Chow Mein

MAKES 4 SERVINGS

- ¾ pound chicken thighs, cut into ¾-inch cubes
- 1 tablespoon soy sauce
- 1 tablespoon cornstarch
- 3 tablespoons vegetable oil, divided
- 1 cup bean sprouts
- 1 cup broccoli florets
- ½ cup fresh or canned sliced bamboo shoots
- ½ cup sliced carrots
- ¼ cup canned sliced water chestnuts
- 8 to 10 snow peas, trimmed
- ½ cup Master Sauce (page 224)
- Crispy Chow Mein Noodles (recipe follows), for serving

This dish always caused "lost in translation" moments. In Chinese, when we use the term "chow mein"—or *chao mian* in Mandarin—we are talking about stir-fried boiled noodles. But what our customers wanted when they said "chicken chow mein" was this chop suey mix of vegetables and chicken, sprinkled with crispy chow mein noodles. I recall so many exchanges with diners to clarify their orders. We finally decided to spell it out and distinguish the two by calling one chow mein and the other "Chinese-style stir-fried noodles." To make the crispy chow mein noodles, we cut wonton skins into strips and deep-fried them. People would order extra bags of the noodles to eat like chips.

■ In a medium bowl, put the chicken and soy sauce, and mix to combine. Add the cornstarch and mix well. Set aside.

■ Preheat a wok over high heat until wisps of smoke rise from the surface. Add 2 tablespoons of the oil and heat until it starts to shimmer. Add the chicken and stir-fry for 2 to 3 minutes, or until the chicken is nearly cooked through. Remove the wok from the heat, transfer the chicken to a medium bowl, and set aside. Rinse the wok and dry with a towel.

■ Return the wok to the stove over high heat. Add the remaining 1 tablespoon oil and heat until it starts to shimmer. Add the sprouts, broccoli, bamboo shoots, carrots, water chestnuts, and peas, and stir-fry for 1 to 2 minutes, or until the broccoli has started to turn dark green. Add the master sauce and chicken, and stir-fry for 1 to 2 minutes more to coat. Serve topped with the noodles.

→

Crispy Chow Mein Noodles

MAKES ABOUT 2 CUPS

10 pieces wonton wrappers (see note)

1 cup vegetable oil

You could fry just enough crispy noodles to make a batch of Chicken Chow Mein or you could fry the whole pack of wonton skins to make enough fried noodles for a party snack. It's up to you.

■ Take a stack of about 10 wrappers and slice them into strips about ⅓ inch wide. Separate the strips and make sure none of them are stuck together.

■ Line a plate with a few layers of paper towels.

■ In a medium pot over medium-high heat, add the oil and heat until it registers 325 degrees F on an instant-read thermometer. Fry the noodles in batches for about 2 minutes, or until golden brown. Transfer the noodles to the prepared paper towel–lined dinner plate to drain.

NOTE: If you decide to fry the entire pack of wonton wrappers, you can snack on the leftover noodles plain, or, while the noodles are still warm from frying, you can sprinkle them with sugar to taste for a sweet treat.

春捲

Restaurant-Style Egg Rolls

MAKES ABOUT 1 DOZEN

- 2 tablespoons vegetable oil, plus more for frying
- 3 cups thinly sliced green cabbage
- 1 cup shredded carrots
- 1 cup thinly sliced celery
- 3 stalks green onions, cut into 2-inch segments
- 3 tablespoons soy sauce
- Kosher salt (optional)
- ¼ teaspoon sesame oil
- 1 package egg roll wrappers
- 1 egg, beaten
- Sweet-and-Sour Sauce (recipe follows), for serving

Egg rolls were a workhorse appetizer at our restaurant. Customers expected their meals to come with an egg roll. Since our lunch menu featured dishes that were under four dollars and came with fried rice, the egg roll was essentially free. The ingredients, as a result, were humble. Sadly, the flavor almost didn't matter, because people had the habit of drowning the egg rolls in pungent mustard, sweet-and-sour sauce, or soy sauce. Unlike spring roll wrappers, which are thinner, spongy, and more crepe-like, egg roll wrappers are thicker, bubble up when fried, and have a chewy texture. I prefer the more flavorful filling and the crispness of Spring Rolls (page 100), but I include this recipe as a nod to nostalgia.

▪ Preheat a wok over high heat until wisps of smoke rise from the surface. Add 2 tablespoons of the vegetable oil and heat until it shimmers. Add the cabbage, carrots, celery, and onions. Stir-fry the vegetables for about 1 minute, then add the soy sauce. Continue to stir-fry for 3 to 4 minutes, or until the cabbage and carrots are cooked through and soft. Add a pinch of salt to taste. Drizzle with the sesame oil. Give everything a good toss to combine. Set aside to cool for a few minutes.

▪ Position an egg roll wrapper with a corner toward you so that it's like a diamond. Place about ¼ cup filling about 2 inches above the bottom corner of the wrapper. Fold the bottom corner up over the filling and roll it about halfway up. You will have a triangular shape with a bump in the middle. Fold the right-side "flap" over the filling, then the left side. It will look like a bulky envelope. Brush the top flap with egg and then finish rolling to seal. Repeat with the remaining wrappers and filling.

▪ Line a plate with several layers of paper towels. Set aside.

▪ In a deep pan, add about 1½ inches of oil. Heat the oil until it registers 375 degrees F on an instant-read thermometer. Fry the egg rolls in two batches, turning the rolls halfway through, about 2 minutes per side, or until the skin is evenly brown. Transfer the rolls to the prepared paper towel–lined plate. Serve immediately with the Sweet-and-Sour Sauce.

Sweet-and-Sour Sauce

MAKES ABOUT 1 CUP

⅓ cup ketchup

⅓ cup sugar, plus more as needed

⅓ cup white vinegar

This is the recipe for our house sweet-and-sour sauce. People called it "red sauce" because of the color (we used to add a dash of red food coloring). Here, I've opted to leave out the food coloring. I also left out the thickening agent. This is a small enough portion that the sugar and the ketchup add enough thickness to the sauce.

■ In a small pot over medium heat, combine the ketchup, sugar, and vinegar, and stir until the sugar dissolves and the sauce becomes syrupy and slightly thickened, about 5 to 7 minutes. Add a little more sugar, if desired, then let cool and serve. Store leftover sauce in a covered jar in the refrigerator for up to 1 week.

腰果雞

Cashew Chicken

MAKES 4 SERVINGS

¾ pound chicken thighs, cut into ¾-inch cubes
1 tablespoon soy sauce
3 tablespoons cornstarch, divided
3 tablespoons vegetable oil, divided
2 tablespoons water
1 medium stalk celery, sliced into ½-inch-thick pieces (about ½ cup)
½ cup sliced fresh or canned bamboo shoots
½ cup toasted unsalted cashews
½ cup Master Sauce (recipe follows)

Suggested pairing: Restaurant-Style Egg Rolls (page 221).

My mother cooked so much cashew chicken at the restaurant that it probably paid for my college education. For the vegetable, we used celery, which tastes great stir-fried. We bought raw cashews in bulk that we then browned in the deep fryer. For home cooks, I suggest toasting cashews in a dry skillet over medium heat. Alternatively, you can buy toasted unsalted cashews.

- In a medium bowl, put the chicken and soy sauce, and mix to combine. Add 1 tablespoon of the cornstarch and mix well.

- Preheat a wok over high heat until wisps of smoke rise from the surface. Add 2 tablespoons of the oil and heat until it starts to shimmer. Add the chicken and stir-fry for about 2 minutes, or until nearly cooked through. Remove the wok from the heat, transfer the chicken to a medium bowl, and set aside. Rinse the wok and dry with a towel.

- In a small bowl, put the remaining 2 tablespoons cornstarch and the water, and mix to combine. Set aside.

- Return the wok to the stove over high heat. Add the remaining 1 tablespoon oil and heat until it starts to shimmer. Add the celery and stir-fry for about 1 minute to cook through. Add the bamboo shoots, cashews, and chicken, and stir to combine. Add the Master Sauce and stir-fry for about 30 seconds more. Slowly add the cornstarch mixture as you stir the sauce. Continue stirring and gently tossing for 1 to 2 minutes more to combine the thickened sauce with the chicken and vegetables. Serve with steamed or fried rice.

→

Master Sauce

MAKES ABOUT 1¼ CUP

- 1 cup water
- 1 tablespoon finely minced garlic
- 1 tablespoon hoisin sauce
- 1 tablespoon oyster sauce
- 1 tablespoon rice wine, vermouth, or any dry white wine you have on hand
- 1 tablespoon soy sauce
- 1 stalk green onion, finely chopped

The Master Sauce is what we called the universal stir-fry sauce at the restaurant. We would make gallons of it and ladle just enough for each stir-fry. This makes enough for two to three stir-fries.

■ In a small pot over high heat, put the water, garlic, hoisin, oyster sauce, wine, soy sauce, and onions, and stir to combine. Bring the mixture just to a boil, then remove the pot from the heat. You can use the sauce immediately or let it cool and store it in the refrigerator, covered, for up to 4 days.

蟹角

Crab Rangoon

MAKES ABOUT 20 CRAB RANGOONS

- 1 (8-ounce) package cream cheese
- ¼ cup cooked crab meat
- Kosher salt and white pepper powder
- 1 package wonton wrappers
- Vegetable oil, for frying
- 1 cup Sweet-and-Sour Sauce (page 222)

There are a few Americanized dishes that may have some basis in traditional Chinese cooking. This is not one of them. It's said that crab rangoon was created by the Polynesian restaurant chain Trader Vic's. Its popularity quickly spread across Asian eateries as customer demand for these deep-fried pouches of cream cheese ballooned. We didn't serve crab rangoon for many years, which disappointed many of our diners. We didn't even know what it was at first. Eventually, we gave in and put it on the menu, knowing that once we'd made the decision, we'd never be able to go back. Each batch of filling weighed in at nearly ten pounds. That's a lot of cream cheese.

■ In a medium bowl, put the cream cheese, crab meat, and salt and pepper to taste, and mix well.

■ Place about 1 tablespoon of filling in the middle of a wonton wrapper. Fold the wrapper into a triangle, dab the edges with water, and seal it to create a pouch. Repeat with the remaining wrappers and filling. Alternatively, for a prettier method, you can cinch together the edges of the wonton wrapper to create a four-pointed star. Estimate the midpoint of each edge of the wonton square and then "pin" the midpoint of the wrapper edge to the center of the mound of filling. Repeat with the other edges. You can shimmy the edges together, using the cream cheese as glue. Repeat with the remaining wrappers and filling.

■ Line a plate with several layers of paper towels. Set aside.

■ In a large Dutch oven over medium-high heat, heat the oil until it registers 325 degrees F on an instant-read thermometer. Fry the crab rangoon in batches until golden brown, 1 to 2 minutes. Transfer the crab rangoon to the prepared paper towel–lined plate to drain. Serve hot with the Sweet-and-Sour Sauce.

素十錦

Vegetarian's Delight

MAKES 4 SERVINGS

- 1 tablespoon vegetable oil
- ¾ pound mixed leafy greens, such as baby bok choy and Chinese cabbage, cut into bite-size chunks
- 6 to 8 snow peas, trimmed
- ¼ cup thinly sliced carrot rounds
- 8 pieces canned baby corn
- 2 tablespoons water
- 2 medium cloves garlic, finely minced
- 1 to 2 tablespoons soy sauce
- ¼ teaspoon sesame oil

You often see incarnations of stir-fried mixed vegetables in Asian restaurants. My father coined "vegetarian's delight" to describe our version. I think he was trying to apply Chinese logic and confer some lyricism into the name of this dish. Alas, English isn't as concise as the Chinese language when it comes to imbuing poetry in a few characters. The particular mix of vegetables is up to you.

■ Preheat a wok over high heat until wisps of smoke rise from the surface. Add the oil and heat until it starts to shimmer. Add the greens, and toss and stir to wilt them. Add the peas, carrots, and corn. Stir-fry for 1 to 2 minutes more. Add the water, garlic, and soy sauce. Stir and toss to combine, continuing to stir-fry until the greens have wilted and don't look raw, about 1 to 2 minutes. The timing can vary slightly depending on the type of vegetable you're using. Drizzle on the sesame oil. Serve with rice.

蒙古牛

Mongolian Beef

MAKES 4 SERVINGS

- 1 pound flank steak
- 4 tablespoons soy sauce, divided
- 2 teaspoons cornstarch
- 3 tablespoons vegetable oil, divided
- 2 or 3 dried red chili peppers (optional)
- 3 stalks green onions, cut into 2½-inch segments
- ½ medium yellow onion, cut into ⅛-inch-thick slices
- 1 heaping tablespoon sweet bean sauce
- 1 tablespoon water
- Fried "Rice Stick" Noodles (recipe follows), for serving (optional)

My husband finds pleasure in going to Chinese restaurants where he's the only Caucasian diner in a sea of Asians. He will gnaw on chicken feet, eat pig's ear at dim sum restaurants, and make his best attempts at ordering beer in Mandarin. But when he sees Mongolian beef on a menu, he will order it sheepishly and devour it with a copious amount of rice. At the restaurant, we would serve Mongolian beef over a pile of fried "rice stick" noodles. I typically don't bother with the noodles when I make this at home since it's more for effect than flavor. The directions for frying the noodles follow, if you prefer to serve the beef with the noodles as a base.

▪ Trim the flank steak of any large pieces of membrane. Cut the flank in half or thirds lengthwise, or with the grain. Depending on the total width of the flank, you may get two or three sections that are about 3 inches wide. Cut these sections against the grain into ⅛-inch slices. Place the beef in a medium bowl. Add 2 tablespoons of the soy sauce and mix well. Add the cornstarch and mix well again.

▪ Preheat a wok over high heat until wisps of smoke rise from the surface. Add 2 tablespoons of the oil and heat until it starts to shimmer. Add the beef and stir-fry for 1 to 2 minutes, or until the beef has browned and is nearly cooked through. Remove the wok from the heat, transfer the beef to a medium bowl, and set aside.

▪ Return the wok to the stove over high heat. Add the remaining 1 tablespoon oil and the chilies. Stir-fry for about 10 seconds. Add the green and yellow onions, making sure to break up the yellow onion slices with a spatula, and stir-fry for 2 to 3 minutes, or until the onions have begun to soften and cook down. Add the remaining 2 tablespoons soy sauce, the bean sauce, and water, and mix. Add the beef and stir-fry for 2 to 3 minutes more, or until the sauce has coated the beef and onions. Serve with the Fried "Rice Stick" Noodles.

→

Fried "Rice Stick" Noodles

MAKES A MOUND OF NOODLES

2 cups vegetable oil

1 fistful rice-stick noodles (see note)

Look for the rice noodles that are labeled "rice stick," usually sold in one-pound packages. The noodles puff up quite a bit, so you will need only a fraction of a package of noodles. Store the unused noodles in a ziplock bag in the pantry.

- Line a plate with several layers of paper towels, and set aside.

- In a medium Dutch oven over medium-high heat, heat the oil until it registers 350 degrees F on an instant-read thermometer. Carefully lower the bundle of noodles into the oil. It will immediately puff up and turn white. Let it fry for 10 to 15 seconds. Using tongs, flip the whole mess of noodles to fry the other side for another 10 to 15 seconds. Transfer the noodles to the plate to drain. Place the fried noodles on a platter and arrange the Mongolian Beef on top.

NOTE: The noodles are dried in tight, flat bundles that are hard to break. You will have to tug a fistful of noodles that measures roughly 1 inch in diameter from one of the bundles. Shards of loose noodles will likely fall all over the place.

蝦龍糊

Shrimp With "Lobster Sauce"

(Dong Ting Shrimp)

MAKES 4 SERVINGS

- ¾ pound raw shrimp (size 16/20), peeled and deveined
- 1½ teaspoons kosher salt, divided
- 2 egg whites, divided
- 1 tablespoon plus 2 teaspoons cornstarch, divided
- 2 tablespoons vegetable oil, divided
- About 1 cup water, divided
- 1 cup broccoli florets
- ¼ cup thinly sliced carrot rounds
- 8 to 10 snow peas, trimmed
- 6 pieces canned baby corn
- 1 tablespoon Shaoxing wine or dry Marsala wine
- ⅛ teaspoon white pepper powder
- ¼ teaspoon sesame oil

Suggested pairings: Kung Pao Chicken (page 151) or Simple Stir-Fried Greens (page 137).

Named after Lake Dong Ting near the Hunan Province, this shrimp with vegetables in a velvety egg-white sauce was our shrimp in "lobster sauce" surrogate. We figured that shrimp in lobster sauce was something created for Westerners, but we'd never had it and didn't know what it looked like, so we offered this version. I like the combination of the lighter flavor and rich texture.

▪ In a medium bowl, put the shrimp, ½ teaspoon of the salt, and 1 egg white, and mix well. Add 2 teaspoons of the cornstarch and mix well again.

▪ Preheat a wok over medium-high heat until wisps of smoke rise from the surface. Add 1 tablespoon of the vegetable oil and heat until it starts to shimmer. Add the coated shrimp and quickly stir-fry to parcook the shrimp, about 1 to 2 minutes. The outside will be pink, but the inside won't be fully cooked. Remove the wok from the heat and transfer the shrimp to a medium bowl. Set aside.

▪ In a small bowl, combine 2 tablespoons of the water with the remaining 1 tablespoon cornstarch. Set aside. In a liquid measuring cup, beat the remaining 1 egg white with 1 teaspoon of the water. Set aside. Rinse the wok and dry with a towel.

▪ Return the wok to the stove over high heat. Add the remaining 1 tablespoon vegetable oil and heat until it starts to shimmer. Add the broccoli, carrots, peas, and corn, and stir-fry for 1 to 2 minutes, or until the broccoli has turned a dark green. Add the remaining 1 teaspoon salt, ½ cup of the water, and the wine, and stir to combine.

▪ Add the shrimp to the vegetables. Stir-fry for 2 minutes, or until the sauce thickens slightly and the shrimp have finished cooking. (You do not want to overcook the shrimp.) If it looks like there isn't enough sauce, add about ¼ cup water, or more if necessary. Add the cornstarch slurry and stir to combine. Drizzle the egg white into the sauce in as thin a stream as you can to create threads, and stir. Remove the pan from the heat. Finish with the white pepper and sesame oil. Serve with steamed rice.

左公雞

General Tso's Chicken

MAKES 4 SERVINGS

¼ cup soy sauce

1 stalk green onions, finely chopped

1 tablespoon sugar

2 cloves garlic, finely minced

1½ pounds boneless chicken thighs

Vegetable oil, for frying

About 2 cups cornstarch

For the sauce:

¼ cup plus 3 tablespoons water, divided

3 tablespoons cornstarch

1 tablespoon vegetable oil

1 teaspoon red pepper flakes

¼ cup soy sauce

3 tablespoons white vinegar

2 tablespoons strawberry jam

1 tablespoon sugar

Suggested pairing: Simple Stir-Fried Greens (page 137).

I always say that there's nothing inherently wrong with crispy chicken cutlets in a thick, spicy, sticky-sweet, and salty sauce, but General Tso's chicken isn't Chinese. (There is a documentary about this topic called *The Search for General Tso*.) It does have the spirit of Chinese cooking, in that it combines textures and balances flavors, which is why it works. While it may not be authentic to Chinese cuisine, this dish is delicious. Because customers demanded General Tso's chicken, we had to figure out how to make it. My father, who loved strawberry jam, decided on a whim to add it to the sauce. We also served a mild version of this dish called Strawberry Chicken. Customers loved it.

▪ In a large bowl, put the soy sauce, onions, sugar, and garlic, and stir to combine. Set aside.

▪ Cut the chicken into pieces about 2 inches long and 1 inch wide. Add the chicken to the soy sauce marinade and stir to coat. Cover or transfer to a ziplock bag and marinate for at least 30 minutes or up to overnight.

▪ Line a plate with several layers of paper towels. Set aside.

▪ Place about 1½ inches of vegetable oil in a medium Dutch oven over medium-high heat. Heat the oil until it registers 350 degrees F on an instant-read thermometer. Dredge the marinated chicken pieces in the cornstarch. Fry the chicken in batches, stirring carefully to ensure even frying, for 3 to 5 minutes, or until golden brown. Transfer the chicken to the prepared paper towel–lined plate. Set aside.

▪ To make the sauce, in a small bowl, combine 3 tablespoons of the water with the cornstarch. Set aside.

▪ In a medium saucepan over medium heat, heat the oil and pepper flakes. Add the soy sauce, vinegar, jam, sugar, and the remaining ¼ cup water, and stir to combine. Bring to a simmer, stirring to dissolve the jam and sugar. Gradually whisk in the cornstarch slurry to thicken the sauce. You may not need all of the slurry. Let the sauce simmer for about 1 minute, or until the sauce darkens and starts to glisten. Remove the pan from the heat.

▪ Add the chicken pieces to the sauce, and toss to combine. Serve with rice.

芥藍雞

Beef with Broccoli

MAKES 4 SERVINGS

½ pound flank steak

2 tablespoons plus 1½ teaspoons soy sauce, divided, plus more as needed

1 teaspoon finely minced fresh ginger

1 teaspoon Shaoxing wine or dry Marsala wine

2 medium cloves garlic, crushed

1 tablespoon plus 1½ teaspoons cornstarch

1 tablespoon vegetable oil

2 heaping cups broccoli florets, blanched for about 2 minutes and drained

2 to 3 tablespoons water

1 teaspoon hoisin sauce

¼ teaspoon sesame oil

Suggested pairings: Chicken with Snow Peas (page 153) or Vegetarian's Delight (page 226).

This dish is so ubiquitous and straightforward that it may seem "boring." But I actually enjoy beef (or chicken) with broccoli. At the restaurant, we used the Master Sauce (page 224) for this dish. Here, I offer my home-style version, which infuses more flavor into the beef itself. If you don't like regular broccoli, you certainly can use Chinese broccoli. For Chinese broccoli, you will need to roughly chop the leaves and then peel the thick stems and cut them into thin slices.

■ Trim the flank steak of any large pieces of membrane. Cut the flank in half or thirds lengthwise, or with the grain. Depending on the total width of the flank, you may get two or three sections that are about 3 inches wide. Cut these sections against the grain into ⅛-inch slices. Place the beef in a medium bowl. Add 1 tablespoon of the soy sauce, the ginger, wine, and garlic, and mix well. Add the cornstarch, and mix well again.

■ Preheat a wok over high heat until wisps of smoke rise from the surface. Add the vegetable oil and heat until it starts to shimmer. Gently add the beef and, using a spatula, spread it into a single layer in the bowl of the wok. Sear it for about 30 seconds and then stir-fry for 1 to 2 minutes, or until the meat has browned. Add the broccoli, water, remaining 1 tablespoon plus 1½ teaspoons soy sauce, and the hoisin, and stir-fry for 1 to 2 minutes, or until the sauce has thickened slightly. Add a dash more soy sauce, if desired. Drizzle with the sesame oil and serve with steamed rice.

木樨肉

Mu Shu Pork

MAKES 4 TO 6 SERVINGS

- 2 tablespoons vegetable oil, divided
- 1 large egg, beaten
- 2 tablespoons water
- 1 tablespoon plus 1½ teaspoons sweet bean sauce
- 1 tablespoon oyster sauce
- 1 tablespoon Shaoxing wine or dry Marsala wine
- 1 tablespoon soy sauce
- 6 mu shu pancakes (see note)
- 2 stalks green onions, roughly chopped
- 4 cups thinly sliced green cabbage, loosely packed
- ⅓ pound Chinese barbecued pork, julienned (about 1½ cup)
- 1 cup bean sprouts
- ¼ teaspoon sesame oil
- ⅛ teaspoon white pepper powder
- 3 teaspoons hoisin sauce, for serving

The origins of this dish are not clear. But in China, mu shu pork is a stir-fry that includes wood ear fungus, eggs, and cucumber, and is served with rice. *Mu* is short for *mu er*, or "wood ear," and *shu* refers to sweet osmanthus flower, which is used as a poetic description of the eggs. Once the dish made it to America, green cabbage took the place of cucumber and tortilla-like pancakes took the place of rice. At our restaurant, mu shu was a popular dish—mostly because people liked using the pancakes to roll up the filling like a burrito and also because we used our house-made barbecued pork (*cha shao* or *char siu*). You can make the barbecued pork yourself (see page 239) or you can buy some from your favorite Chinese barbecue shop.

■ Preheat a wok over medium-high heat until wisps of smoke rise from the surface. Add 1 tablespoon of the vegetable oil and heat until it starts to shimmer. Add the egg and scramble it, cooking until the curd is just set, about 1 to 2 minutes. Remove the wok from the heat, transfer the egg to a small bowl, and set aside.

■ In a small bowl or measuring cup, put the water, bean sauce, oyster sauce, wine, and soy sauce, and stir to combine. Set aside.

■ Set up your steamer (see page 47) to steam the pancakes. Steam the pancakes for 5 to 7 minutes, or until heated through and softened.

■ While the pancakes are steaming, heat the wok over high heat until wisps of smoke rise from the surface. Add the remaining 1 tablespoon vegetable oil and the onions, and stir-fry for 10 to 15 seconds. Add the cabbage, pork, and bean sprouts, and stir to combine. Add the bean sauce mixture, using a spatula if needed to scrape down the sides of the bowl. Stir-fry the filling together for 1 to 2 minutes, or until the cabbage has softened. Add the sesame oil and pepper, and stir and toss again to combine. Remove the wok from the heat.

■ Spread ½ teaspoon hoisin sauce into the middle of each pancake. Add about ½ cup of the filling to each and roll the pancakes up like a burrito to serve.

NOTE: Mu shu pancakes are typically sold frozen. Let them defrost in the refrigerator overnight before steaming.

中式叉燒肉

Chinese Barbecued Pork

MAKES ABOUT 1 POUND

- 1 to 1¼ pound pork tenderloin
- 2 tablespoons red fermented bean curd (optional)
- 2 tablespoons soy sauce
- 1 tablespoon plus 1½ teaspoons honey
- 1 heaping tablespoon hoisin sauce
- 1 tablespoon oyster sauce
- 3 to 4 large cloves garlic, crushed

Most of the barbecued pork you find in Chinese restaurants or barbecue shops is made with red dye to mimic the color that traditionally would come from the addition of red fermented bean curd, which achieves its ruddiness from a fermented red rice. If you can get to a well-stocked Asian market, look for "red bean curd," which is not to be confused with fermented tofu or bean curd with chili. Red bean curd is often used in marinades and adds dimension. If you can't find it, leave it out. Serve this barbecued pork as an appetizer or use in Fried Rice (page 115) or Mu Shu Pork (page 236).

▪ Trim the pork tenderloin of any large pieces of membrane. Cut the tenderloin in half lengthwise. Set aside.

▪ In a small bowl, put the bean curd, soy sauce, honey, hoisin, oyster sauce, and garlic, and stir to combine. Place the tenderloin strips in a large ziplock bag. Add the marinade and seal. Squish it around to make sure each piece of pork gets thoroughly covered in the marinade. Marinate in the refrigerator for at least 3 hours or up to overnight.

▪ Preheat the oven to 425 degrees F. Cover a baking sheet with foil. Place a heatproof cooling rack onto the baking sheet and place the pork on the rack. Roast the pork in the oven for 30 to 35 minutes, or until the internal temperature of the pork registers 145 to 150 degrees F on an instant-read thermometer. Let rest for 5 minutes before slicing, and serve.

杏仁豆腐

Almond Jelly with Fruit Cocktail

MAKES 4 TO 6 SERVINGS

2 (¼-ounce) envelopes Knox gelatin

¼ cup sugar

1½ cups water

1 tablespoon almond extract

1 cup low-fat milk

1 (15-ounce) can fruit cocktail in syrup, chilled

The Chinese love to eat this almond-flavored gelatin with fresh fruit or sweet osmanthus syrup (which is made from osmanthus flowers; osmanthus is also used to flavor tea). It's said that the almond extract in the gelatin has cooling properties for the body to combat hot weather. Restaurants often serve almond jelly—also called almond tofu, because it looks like tofu—with canned fruit cocktail or lychees in syrup. I especially loved eating almond jelly because it was paired with fruit cocktail. If you want to get fancy, use mixed tropical fruit cocktail.

■ In a medium heatproof bowl, combine the gelatin and sugar. Set aside.

■ In a small pot over high heat, bring the water to a boil. Remove from the heat. Add the water to the gelatin mixture and stir until it dissolves. Add the almond extract and milk, and stir to combine. Pour the gelatin mixture into an 8-by-8-inch square baking dish and chill for at least 4 hours or up to overnight. Alternatively, you can chill the gelatin in four to six dessert bowls.

■ To serve, cut the gelatin into cubes and divide it between four to six bowls. Divide the fruit cocktail and syrup among the bowls of gelatin, and serve.

Acknowledgments

They say that stories happen only to those who can tell them. Were I not born to two journalists, I would not have developed a "nose for news" and the instinct to tell stories. My parents took a great leap of faith to move us from Taiwan to the United States. They jumped again and again with each decision that determined the trajectory of our lives. That journey eventually led me here. To my late father, Chou Chang-Sheng, and my mother, Shyu Huann-Ming, I pay the most profound tribute.

To my husband, Eric Riddle, who told me on our first date that he appreciates a strong woman and who saw me for me—I am yours. He balances all of my drive with his goofy sense of humor, which, thankfully, he has passed on to our children. While I was writing this book, he had a sixth sense about when to call for pizza or bring home teriyaki, because he suspected I had no energy left to make dinner for our family. He is also our family's dishwasher in chief, which was especially crucial when I was testing recipes. Our home would not be a home without him.

Thank you to my daughter, Meilee, and my son, Shen, for being patient with me while I focused on making this book. I lost count of how many times I shushed them for being too loud or the number of nights I confined myself to the quietest corner of the house to write instead of spend time with them. Kids, I hope you're proud of me.

Thank you to my editor, Susan Roxborough, for being persistent about signing me and saving me from my own ambition to self-publish. Her impact on the production quality of books at Sasquatch is indisputable. The Sasquatch team—Anna Goldstein, Tony Ong, and Em Gale—have worked their magic.

Clare Barboza, photographer extraordinaire, said "yes" before I could finish asking her to shoot the images for this book. She agreed even though, at the time, I was going to self-publish and hadn't yet secured funding. While we ultimately didn't have to crowdfund, I am humbled by her trust and, more importantly, her artistry.

Thank you to Grace Young, Steven Raichlen, Bruce Aidells, Naomi Duguid, and Deborah Madison for their generosity.

I enlisted friends and some of my students at Hot Stove Society to test recipes. I wanted the widest range of cooks, and I got them. Many thanks to: Lynn Abolofia, Judy Amster, Michi Broman, Jaimie Carde, Bridget Charters, Darryl Dayton, Alisa Dorion, Teresa Engrav, Lisa Gallo, Shannon Gee, Lisa Hale, Lindsey Jackson, Jennifer Johnson, Alexandra Laing, Jennifer Lau, Kellie Leake, Michelle Locke, Rebekkah Madden, Teresa Mainieri, Brenda Pederson, Tracy Pegg, Ryan Phee, Chris Plaisier, Marc Schermerhorn, Traci Tenneson, Sherry Toly, Colleen Wadden, Kairu Yao, Christine Yorozu, and Jill W.

Special thanks to Dawn Smith for sampling more soy sauces than any one person should and sharing your erudite tasting notes, and to Cindy Kutner, who not only tested recipes, but has supported me since my days at the *Denver Post*. Before I left Denver in 2000, she gifted me a bookmark engraved with "For The Book." I will now, finally, be able to use that bookmark.

Index

Note: Photographs are indicated by *italics*.

E

F

G

R

S

T

V

W

X

Y

Z

Conversions

VOLUME			LENGTH		WEIGHT	
UNITED STATES	METRIC	IMPERIAL	UNITED STATES	METRIC	AVOIRDUPOIS	METRIC
¼ tsp.	1.25 ml		⅛ in.	3 mm	¼ oz.	7 g
½ tsp.	2.5 ml		¼ in.	6 mm	½ oz.	15 g
1 tsp.	5 ml		½ in.	1.25 cm	1 oz.	30 g
½ Tbsp.	7.5 ml		1 in.	2.5 cm	2 oz.	60 g
1 Tbsp.	15 ml		1 ft.	30 cm	3 oz.	90 g
⅛ c.	30 ml	1 fl. oz.			4 oz.	115 g
¼ c.	60 ml	2 fl. oz.			5 oz.	150 g
⅓ c.	80 ml	2.5 fl. oz.			6 oz.	175 g
½ c.	125 ml	4 fl. oz.			7 oz.	200 g
1 c.	250 ml	8 fl. oz.			8 oz. (½ lb.)	225 g
2 c. (1 pt.)	500 ml	16 fl. oz.			9 oz.	250 g
1 qt.	1 l	32 fl. oz.			10 oz.	300 g
TEMPERATURE					11 oz.	325 g
OVEN MARK	FAHRENHEIT	CELSIUS	GAS		12 oz.	350 g
Very cool	250–275	130–140	½–1		13 oz.	375 g
Cool	300	150	2		14 oz.	400 g
Warm	325	165	3		15 oz.	425 g
Moderate	350	175	4		16 oz. (1 lb.)	450 g
Moderately hot	375	190	5		1½ lb.	750 g
	400	200	6		2 lb.	900 g
Hot	425	220	7		2¼ lb.	1 kg
	450	230	8		3 lb.	1.4 kg
Very Hot	475	245	9		4 lb.	1.8 kg

About the Author

Award-winning food journalist, cooking instructor, and former restaurateur **Hsiao-Ching Chou** grew up immersed in storytelling and food culture. Her immigrant family opened a restaurant in Missouri when she was eight years old. She worked there after school and on weekends for the next sixteen years until she graduated from the University of Missouri's School of Journalism.

She spent more than a decade as a newspaper food writer and editor, first at the *Denver Post* and then at the *Seattle Post-Intelligencer*. She received the coveted Bert Greene Award for Excellence in Food Writing from the International Association for Culinary Professionals for her feature article about traveling to Cordova, Alaska, to profile a native Eyak woman known for making the best smoked Copper River king salmon. Chou has been a guest on local and national shows, including Public Radio's *The Splendid Table* and the Travel Channel's *Anthony Bourdain: No Reservations*. She and her family were among the subjects featured in the PBS documentary *The Meaning of Food*.

In 2011 she pivoted her career to direct the communications program for the renowned Institute for Systems Biology, a nonprofit biomedical research organization in Seattle. In her spare time she teaches everyday Chinese home cooking to students at the Hot Stove Society school. Since 2015 she has been a member of the James Beard Foundation's Cookbook Awards committee, which administers the prestigious annual competition for the best in category cookbooks. She is also a member of Les Dames d'Escoffier. Chou lives in Seattle with her TV-producer husband, two children, and mother. Find her at MyChineseSoulFood.com.

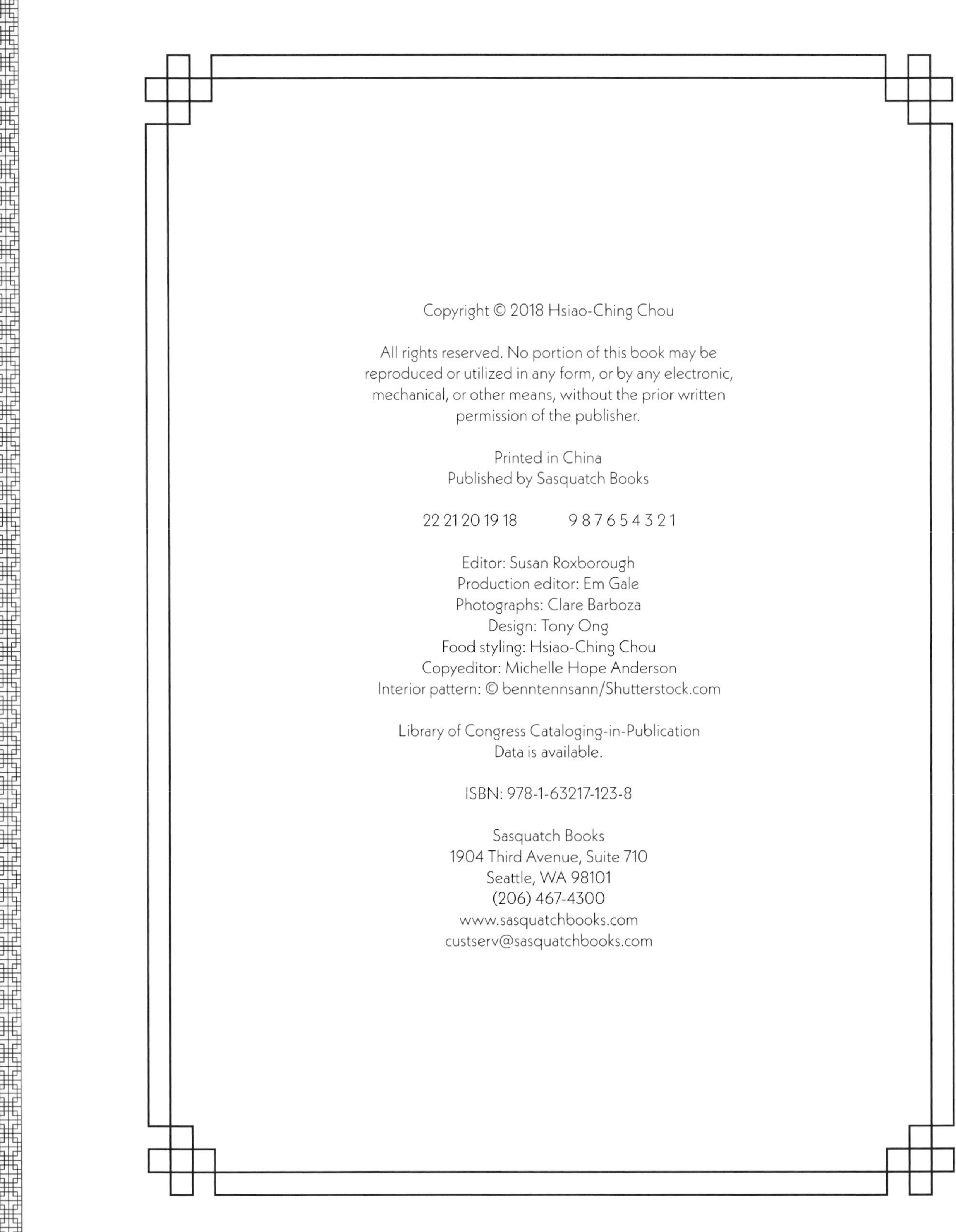

Printed in China
Published by Sasquatch Books

22 21 20 19 18 9 8 7 6 5 4 3 2 1

Editor: Susan Roxborough
Production editor: Em Gale
Photographs: Clare Barboza
Design: Tony Ong
Food styling: Hsiao-Ching Chou
Copyeditor: Michelle Hope Anderson
Interior pattern: © benntennsann/Shutterstock.com

Library of Congress Cataloging-in-Publication
Data is available.

ISBN: 978-1-63217-123-8

Sasquatch Books
1904 Third Avenue, Suite 710
Seattle, WA 98101
(206) 467-4300
www.sasquatchbooks.com
custserv@sasquatchbooks.com